Table of Contents

Introduction

"SEL is the process through which all young people and adults acquire and apply the knowledge, skills, and attitudes to develop healthy identities, manage emotions and achieve personal and collective goals, feel and show empathy for others, establish and maintain supportive relationships, and make responsible and caring decisions." (CASEL 2020)

Social-emotional learning (SEL) covers a wide range of skills that help people improve themselves and get fulfilment from their relationships. They are the skills that help propel us into the people we want to be. SEL skills give people the tools to think about the future and manage the day-to-day goal setting to get where we want to be.

The National Commission for Social, Emotional, and Academic Development (2018) noted that children need many skills, attitudes, and values to succeed in school, future careers, and life. "They require skills such as paying attention, setting goals, collaboration and planning for the future. They require attitudes such as internal motivation, perseverance, and a sense of purpose. They require values such as responsibility, honesty, and integrity. They require the abilities to think critically, consider different views, and problem solve." Explicit SEL instruction will help students develop and hone these important skills, attitudes, and values.

Daniel Goleman (2005), a social scientist who popularized SEL, adds, "Most of us have assumed that the kind of academic learning that goes on in school has little or nothing to do with one's emotions or social environment. Now, neuroscience is telling us exactly the opposite. The emotional centers of the brain are intricately interwoven with the neocortical areas involved in cognitive learning." As adults, we may find it difficult to focus on work after a bad day or a traumatic event. Similarly, student learning is impacted by their emotions. By teaching students how to deal with their emotions in a healthy way, they will reap the benefits academically as well.

SEL is doing the work to make sure students can be successful at home, with their friends, at school, in sports, in relationships, and in life. The skills are typically separated into five competencies: self-awareness, self-management, social awareness, relationship skills, and responsible decision-making.

Introduction *(cont.)*

Social-Emotional Competencies

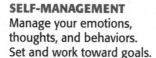

SELF-MANAGEMENT
Manage your emotions, thoughts, and behaviors. Set and work toward goals.

SOCIAL AWARENESS
Take on the perspectives of others, especially those who are different from you. Understand societal expectations and know where to get support.

SELF-AWARENESS
Recognize your own emotions, thoughts, and values. Assess your strengths and weaknesses. Have a growth mindset.

RESPONSIBLE DECISION-MAKING
Make positive choices based on established norms. Understand and consider consequences.

RELATIONSHIP SKILLS
Establish and maintain relationships with others. Communicate effectively and negotiate conflict as necessary.

Each SEL competency helps support child development in life-long learning. SEL helps students develop the skills to have rich connections with their emotional lives and build robust emotional vocabularies. These competencies lead to some impressive data to support students being successful in school and in life.

- Students who learn SEL skills score an average of 11 percentage points higher on standardized tests.

- They are less likely to get office referrals and will spend more time in class.

- These students are more likely to want to come to school and report being happier while at school.

- Educators who teach SEL skills report a 77 percent increase in job satisfaction. (Durlack, et al. 2011)

Your SEL Skills

Educators, parents, and caretakers have a huge part to play as students develop SEL skills. Parker Palmer (2007) reminds us that what children do is often a reflection of what they see and experience. When you stay calm, name your feelings, practice clear communication, and problem-solve in a way that students see, then they reflect that modeling in their own relationships. As you guide students in how to handle conflicts, you can keep a growth mindset and know that with practice, your students can master any skill.

180 Days of Social-Emotional Learning for Sixth Grade

Jennifer Edgerton, Ed.M.

Consultants

Kris Hinrichsen, M.A.T., NBCT
Teacher and Educational Consultant
Anchorage School District

Amy Zoque
Teacher and Instructional Coach
Ontario Montclair School District

Publishing Credits

Corinne Burton, M.A.Ed., *Publisher*
Emily R. Smith, M.A.Ed., *VP of Content Development*
Lynette Ordoñez, *Content Specialist*
David Slayton, *Assistant Editor*
Jill Malcolm, *Multimedia Specialist*

Image Credits: all images from iStock and/or Shutterstock

Social-Emotional Learning Framework

The CASEL SEL framework and competencies were used in the development of this series.
© 2020 The Collaborative for Academic, Social, and Emotional Learning

A division of Teacher Created Materials
5482 Argosy Avenue
Huntington Beach, CA 92649-1039
www.tcmpub.com/shell-education
ISBN 978-1-0876-4975-7
© 2022 Shell Educational Publishing, Inc.

Scenarios

There are many benefits to teaching SEL, from how students behave at home to how they will succeed in life. Let's think about how children with strong SEL skills would react to common life experiences.

At Home

Kyle wakes up. He uses self-talk and says to himself, *I am going to do my best today.* He gets out of bed, picks out his own clothes to wear, and gets ready. As he sits down for breakfast, his little sister knocks over his glass of milk. He thinks, *Uggh, she is so messy! But that's ok—it was just an accident.* Then, he tells his parent and helps clean up the mess.

When his parent picks Kyle up from school, Kyle asks how they are feeling and answers questions about how his day has gone. He says that he found the reading lesson hard, but he used deep breathing and asked questions to figure out new words today.

As his family is getting dinner ready, he sees that his parent is making something he really doesn't like. He stomps his foot in protest, and then he goes to sit in his room for a while. When he comes out, he asks if they can make something tomorrow that he likes.

When he is getting ready for bed, he is silly and playful. He wants to read and point out how each person in the book is feeling. His parent asks him how he would handle the problem the character is facing, and then they talk about the situation.

At School

Cynthia gets to school a little late, and she has to check into the office. Cynthia is embarrassed about being late but feels safe at school and knows that the people there will welcome her with kindness. She steps into her room, and her class pauses to welcome her. Her teacher says, "I'm so glad you are here today."

Cynthia settles into her morning work. After a few minutes, she comes to a problem she doesn't know how to solve. After she gives it her best try, she asks her teacher for some help. Her teacher supports her learning, and Cynthia feels proud of herself for trying.

As lunchtime nears, Cynthia realizes she forgot her lunch in the car. She asks her teacher to call her mom. Her mom says she can't get away and that Cynthia is going to have to eat the school lunch today. Cynthia is frustrated but decides that she is not going to let it ruin her day.

As she is getting ready for school to end, her teacher invites the class to reflect about their day. What is something they are proud of? What is something they wished they could do again? Cynthia thinks about her answers and shares with the class.

These are both pretty dreamy children. The reality is that the development of SEL skills happens in different ways. Some days, students will shock you by how they handle a problem. Other times, they will dig in and not use the skills you teach them. One of the benefits of teaching SEL is that when a student is melting down, your mindset shifts to *I wonder how I can help them learn how to deal with this* rather than *I'm going to punish them so they don't do this again.* Viewing discipline as an opportunity to teach rather than punish is critical for students to learn SEL.

How to Use This Book

Using the Practice Pages

This series is designed to support the instruction of SEL. It is not a curriculum. The activities will help students practice, learn, and grow their SEL skills. Each week is set up for students to practice all five SEL competencies.

 Day 1—Self-Awareness

 Day 2—Self-Management

 Day 3—Social Awareness

 Day 4—Relationship Skills

 Day 5—Responsible Decision-Making

Each of the five competencies has subcategories that are used to target specific skills each day. See the chart on pages 10–11 for a listing of which skills are used throughout the book.

Each week also has a theme. These themes rotate and are repeated several times throughout the book. The following themes are included in this book:

- self
- friends
- family
- community
- school
- state
- country
- world

This book also features one week that focuses on online safety.

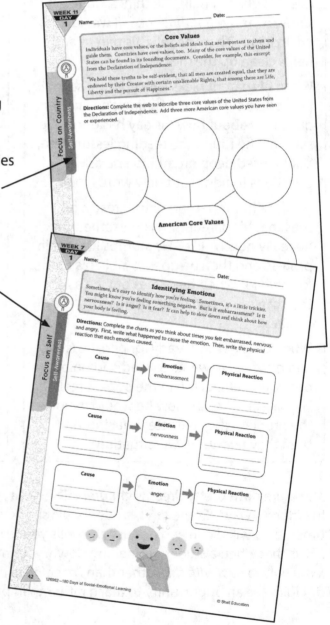

How to Use This Book *(cont.)*

Using the Resources

Rubrics for connecting to self, relating to others, and making decisions can be found on pages 202–204 and in the Digital Resources. Use the rubrics to consider student work. Be sure to share these rubrics with students so that they know what is expected of them.

Diagnostic Assessment

Educators can use the pages in this book as diagnostic assessments. The data analysis tools included with this book enable teachers or parents/caregivers to quickly assess students' work and monitor their progress. Educators can quickly see which skills students may need to target further to develop proficiency.

Students will learn how to connect with their own emotions, how to connect with the emotions of others, and how to make good decisions. Assess student learning in each area using the rubrics on pages 202–204. Then, record their overall progress on the Practice Page Item Analysis sheets on pages 205–207. These charts are also provided in the Digital Resources as PDFs and Microsoft Excel® files.

To Complete the Analyses:

- Write or type students' names in the far-left column. Depending on the number of students, more than one copy of each form may be needed.

- The weeks in which students should be assessed are indicated in the first rows of the charts. Students should be assessed at the ends of those weeks.

- Review students' work for the day(s) indicated in the corresponding rubric. For example, if using the Making Decisions Analysis sheet for the first time, review students' work from Day 5 for all six weeks.

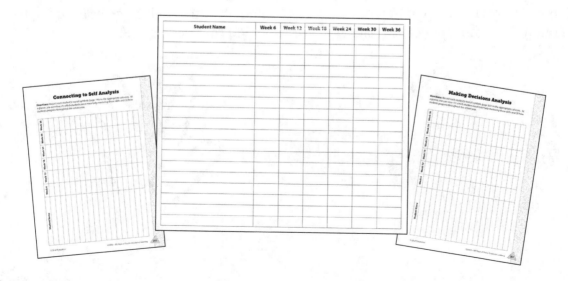

Integrating SEL into Your Teaching

Student self-assessment is key for SEL skills. If students can make accurate evaluations of how they are feeling, then they can work to manage their emotions. If they can manage their emotions, they are more likely to have better relationship skills and make responsible decisions. Children can self-assess from a very young age. The earlier you get them into this practice, the more they will use it and benefit from it for the rest of their lives. The following are some ways you can quickly and easily integrate student self-assessment into your daily routines.

Feelings Check-Ins

Using a scale can be helpful for a quick check-in. After an activity, ask students to rate how they are feeling. Focusing students' attention on how they are feeling helps support their self-awareness. Discuss how students' feelings change as they do different things. Provide students with a visual scale to support these check-ins. These could be taped to their desks or posted in your classroom. Full-color versions of the following scales can be found in the Digital Resources.

- **Emoji:** Having students point to different emoji faces is an easy way to use a rating scale with young students.

- **Symbols:** Symbols, such as weather icons, can also represent students' emotions.

- **Color Wheel:** A color wheel, where different colors represent different emotions, is another effective scale.

- **Numbers:** Have students show 1–5 fingers, with 5 being *I'm feeling great* to 1 being *I'm feeling awful*.

Integrating SEL into Your Teaching (cont.)

Reflection

Reflecting is the process of looking closely or deeply at something. When you prompt students with reflection questions, you are supporting this work. Here is a list of questions to get the reflection process started:

- What did you learn from this work?
- What are you proud of in this piece?
- What would you have done differently?
- What was the most challenging part?
- How could you improve this work?
- How did other people help you finish this work?
- How will doing your best on this assignment help you in the future?

Pan Balance

Have students hold out their arms on both sides of their bodies. Ask them a reflection question that has two possible answers. Students should respond by tipping one arm lower than the other (as if one side of the scale is heavier). Here are some example questions:

- Did you talk too much or too little?
- Were you distracted or engaged?
- Did you rush or take too much time?
- Did you stay calm or get angry?
- Was your response safe or unsafe?

Calibrating Student Assessments

Supporting student self-assessment means calibrating their thinking. You will have students who make mistakes but evaluate themselves as though they have never made a mistake in their lives. At the other end of the spectrum, you will likely see students who will be too hard on themselves. In both these cases, having a periodic calibration can help to support accuracy in their evaluations. The *Calibrating Student Assessments* chart is provided in the Digital Resources (calibrating.pdf).

Teaching Assessment

In addition to assessing students, consider the effectiveness of your own instruction. The *Teaching Rubric* can be found in the Digital Resources (teachingrubric.pdf). Use this tool to evaluate your SEL instruction. You may wish to complete this rubric at different points throughout the year to track your progress.

Skills Alignment

Each activity in this book is aligned to a CASEL competency. Within each competency, students will learn a variety of skills. Here are some of the important skills students will practice during the year.

 Self-Awareness

Identifying Emotions	Core Values
Understanding Different Identities	Developing Interests
Appreciating Cultures	Understanding Strengths and Weaknesses
Honesty	Integrating Identities
Integrity	Examining Stereotypes
Examining Prejudices and Biases	Growth Mindset
Recognizing Assets	Self-Efficacy

 Self-Management

Mindfulness	Time Management
Managing Emotions	Persistence and Perseverance
Collective Care	Self-Motivation
Planning and Organizing	Taking Action
Setting Goals and Milestones	Collective Goals
Stress Management	Self-Discipline
Being Accountable	Personal and Collective Agency

Social Awareness

Taking Others' Perspectives	Compassion
Recognizing Others' Strengths	Appreciating Differences
Empathy	Complimenting Others
Gratitude	Understanding Types of Communication
Influences of Organizations	Sympathy
Understanding Social Norms	Teamwork
Seeking Help	

Skills Alignment *(cont.)*

Relationship Skills

Building New Relationships	Effective Communication
Positive Relationships	Resolving Conflicts
Developing Positive Relationships	Apologizing
Standing Up for Others	Compromise
Leadership	I-Messages
Cultural Competency	Cultural Competency
Nonverbal Communication	Digital Communication

Responsible Decision-Making

Identifying Solutions	Making Decisions
Anticipating Consequences	Evaluating Consequences
Coping with Change	Causes and Effects of Conflicts
Curiosity and Open-Mindedness	Critical Thinking
Making Good Choices	Weighing Options
Identifying Solutions	Weighing Risk and Reward
Resisting Peer Pressure	

Name: _____ Date: _____

Identifying Emotions

Being able to name and express your emotions is key to your happiness and well-being. But emotions can vary in intensity. Sometimes, they are big and overwhelming. Sometimes, they are small and easy to handle.

Directions: For each of the following basic emotions, list at least three words you could use to describe how your mind or body feels. One of them should describe a big feeling, one a medium feeling, and one a small feeling.

Focus on Self
Self-Awareness

Joy

Big: _____

Medium: _____

Small: _____

Anger

Big: _____

Medium: _____

Small: _____

Fear

Big: _____

Medium: _____

Small: _____

Disgust

Big: _____

Medium: _____

Small: _____

Sadness

Big: _____

Medium: _____

Small: _____

Finding Mindfulness

When you are mindful, you are aware of things around you. Mindfulness can be practiced in many ways. You can eat mindfully. You can breathe mindfully. Each of these involves slowing down and paying attention to what is happening in the present. Mindfulness can be a good way to calm down when you are feeling stressed, upset, or angry.

Directions: Read each step, and think about the questions. Close your eyes to get the full experience of sound, smell, and touch. Record your observations.

Sound: What do you hear? Which sounds are nearby? Which are far away? Are you making any sounds?

_____
_____
_____
_____
_____
_____

Touch: What can you feel? Describe the surface you are sitting or lying on. What is the temperature where you are? How comfortable are you?

_____
_____
_____
_____
_____
_____

Smell: What do you smell? Where do you think it is coming from? What does it make you think of?

_____
_____
_____
_____
_____

Sight: Open your eyes, and look all around. What do you see up close? What do you see in the distance? What or who is moving?

_____
_____
_____
_____
_____

Focus on Self

Self-Management

Name: _____ Date: _____

Taking Others' Perspectives

To get along with others, you need to be able to recognize how they are feeling. You need to be able to see things from their perspective. If you respond to a situation without paying attention to how other people are feeling, you may cause hurt feelings or worse. One clue to look for is their body language, or how their face and body look.

Directions: Study the pictures, and describe what might be happening in each situation. How is each person feeling? How do you know?

1.

_____
_____
_____
_____
_____
_____
_____

2.

_____
_____
_____
_____
_____
_____
_____

3.

_____
_____
_____
_____
_____
_____
_____

Name: _____ **Date:** _____

Finding New Relationships

Everyone finds themselves in new places or with new people from time to time. Making friends can be fun, but it can also be hard. Fortunately, there are many things you can do to make new connections with people. Start with a first-step action or friendly words or gestures that can start you down the road to new relationships.

Directions: Read the story. Then, fill the thought bubble with as many first-step actions as you can. If you run out of ideas, ask a partner for help.

Big Changes

It's July. Two weeks ago, Javon moved to a new part of the city. None of his old friends live within walking distance of his home, and his parents are not available to drive him around during the day. Javon noticed that a lot of kids hang out in the park across the street. He also noticed a few kids in his building who don't seem to know many other people. He's bored and lonely at home by himself.

Focus on Self

Relationship Skills

Name:_____ Date:_____

Focus on Self

Responsible Decision-Making

Identifying Solutions

As you get older, you are becoming a more capable problem-solver. Some problems you will face will be small issues, and some will be big problems that require help. Your job is to determine whether each problem is small or big. This will help you decide how to begin to solve it.

Directions: Circle whether each problem is a small one that you can sort out or a big one that requires adult help. If it's a small problem, write what you could do. If it's a big problem, write whom you could ask for help.

1. You just found out that your best friend is having a party and you were not invited.

   big problem   small problem

   _____

2. A friend tells you that he's feeling depressed and has considered harming himself.

   big problem   small problem

   _____

3. As you are leaving math class, you see another student take something from the teacher's drawer.

   big problem   small problem

   _____

4. While playing basketball at the neighborhood court, you see a group of teenagers spray-painting street signs.

   big problem   small problem

   _____

5. When you come home from a walk, the front door to your house is wide open. No one else is home.

   big problem   small problem

   _____

Name: _____ Date: _____

Identifying Your Emotions

Sometimes, it feels like your emotions come out of nowhere. But if you stop and think, you can usually find which events led to your emotional reaction. You may even be able to predict how an action will affect your emotions next time.

Directions: Circle whether each action will make you feel positive or negative emotions. Write why it would affect you in that way.

1. A family member asked you to take out the trash an hour ago. You are in the middle of a tournament for your favorite video game. You decide to ignore their request for now. They probably won't notice until later.

   positive   negative

   _____

   _____

2. You and your sister take turns feeding the cat in the afternoon. Today is your sister's turn. You notice that she is feeling sick when she comes home from school. She immediately falls asleep instead of watching her favorite TV show. You decide to feed the cat today.

   positive   negative

   _____

   _____

3. You forgot to bring your bike inside last night, even though you were reminded. It rained overnight, and the seat is ruined. You decide to hide it behind the bushes so no one will see it.

   positive   negative

   _____

   _____

4. An older family member is coming home from the hospital tomorrow. Your entire family is going to visit her. But you have after-school activities all week. You won't be able to visit her until the weekend. You decide to bake her favorite cookies to send when the rest of your family visits.

   positive   negative

   _____

   _____

Self-Awareness

Focus on Family

Name: _____ **Date:** _____

Managing Your Emotions

Emotions can feel powerful and overwhelming. You can observe them and see where they take you. Or you can use your own thoughts to influence your emotions. You can think of it as self-coaching, self-talk, or simply talking to your brain. Whatever you call it, it's important to keep your messages to yourself positive. Negative self-talk can have a powerful negative effect on your emotions.

Directions: Read each self-talk message. Write whether it makes you feel better or worse and why.

Focus on Family — Self-Management

1. "My brother always gets what he wants, and I never do! I deserve to get *my* way for once!"

_____
_____
_____

2. "It's not fair! My sister does the same thing, and she never gets in trouble. It's like my parents are just waiting for me to make a mistake so they can yell at me."

_____
_____
_____

3. "I forgot to do my chores this morning, but I know I can do better. Everybody makes mistakes sometimes. I'll set a reminder so it doesn't happen again."

_____
_____
_____

Name: _____ Date: _____

Taking Others' Perspectives

We don't always think much about how our family members may be feeling. It's easy to get caught up in our own day-to-day problems and responsibilities. But if you pay attention to your family, you can help when they are feeling down. Consider their words, actions, and how they speak and act.

Focus on Family

Social Awareness

Directions: Read each scenario. Write how each person could help their family member.

1. Maria's brother just got home from school. He slams the door and tosses his backpack in the corner. He walks into the living room and sits down with a big sigh. How could Maria help?

   _____

   _____

   _____

2. Jamie's mom is emptying the dishwasher when there is a crashing sound. Her mom's favorite coffee mug is in pieces on the floor. Jamie's mom leans over the counter and puts her head in her arms. How could Jamie help?

   _____

   _____

   _____

3. Will's grandpa is visiting for a week. Will has been having a great time showing him around. At the end of a long day, Will's grandpa stands up from his chair and yawns. "I think I need a little rest," he says. How could Will help?

   _____

   _____

   _____

4. Dana's older brothers start teasing her for being the baby of the family. Her cheeks get flushed, and she runs out of the room. One of her brothers realizes she's been gone for a few minutes. How could he help Dana?

   _____

   _____

   _____

   _____

Name: _____ Date: _____

Focus on Family

Relationship Skills

Making Positive Relationships

Building positive relationships with your family members is something that you can work on any time. You don't have to wait until something goes wrong or someone needs your help. You and your family members can always do nice things for each other. Small acts of kindness can add up to strong relationships.

Directions: Create ID badges for three family members to show the small ways you could make them feel good.

I.D. BADGE

Name: _____

Favorite activities: _____

Favorite foods: _____

Things that make them smile: _____

_____

Ways I could help them: _____

_____

I.D. BADGE

Name: _____

Favorite activities: _____

Favorite foods: _____

Things that make them smile: _____

_____

Ways I could help them: _____

_____

I.D. BADGE

Name: _____

Favorite activities: _____

Favorite foods: _____

Things that make them smile: _____

_____

Ways I could help them: _____

_____

Name:_____ Date:_____

Anticipating Consequences

Part of making good decisions is thinking about the possible outcomes. What will happen if you make this choice? How will it affect you? How will it affect other people? Being able to anticipate any consequences will help you make more responsible decisions.

Directions: Circle whether each decision will have a positive or negative effect on you. Explain why. Then, name someone else the decision will affect. Circle whether it will have a positive or negative effect on that person. Explain why.

1. You put off a school project until the last minute even though you need a classmate's help on it.

   Effect on you: positive   negative

   _____

   Effect on _____: positive   negative

   _____

2. You make your lunch the night before so you can sleep later in the morning.

   Effect on you: positive   negative

   _____

   Effect on _____: positive   negative

   _____

3. You ask a parent for advice on an argument you're having with a friend.

   Effect on you: positive   negative

   _____

   Effect on _____: positive   negative

   _____

Focus on Family

Responsible Decision-Making

Name: _____ Date: _____

Different Identities

People are all individuals, but they are also members of groups. Most people are born or adopted into family groups. They live in neighborhoods in larger towns or cities. Each family is part of a specific cultural, ethnic, and language group. People may be part of school classrooms, sports teams, or dance groups. They may have close friend groups, regular online gaming parties, or be members of clubs. All of these group identities are part of who a person is.

Directions: Write your name in the center bubble. Write different groups you are a member of in the bubbles. Then, put a star next to the ones that are most important to you.

Focus on Community

Self-Awareness

Collective Care

Whether you live in a big city or a small town, your community works best when everyone pitches in. This is called *collective care*. Everyone can help in both big and small ways. It's important to find ways to take responsibility and help your community.

Directions: How can you help make your community a better place to live? Write or draw at least four specific ways you could help in each category.

Physical Upkeep	Natural Surroundings
People in the Community	**Overall Happiness**

Focus on Community
Self-Management

Name: _____ Date: _____

Recognizing Others' Strengths

There are many people in your community who work hard to make it a better place. They might be teachers, first responders, construction workers, or crossing guards. People help in all kinds of ways. They use their strengths and abilities to help those around them.

Directions: Which two helpers in your community stand out the most? Create an award for each of them. Identify their special contributions by completing the certificates.

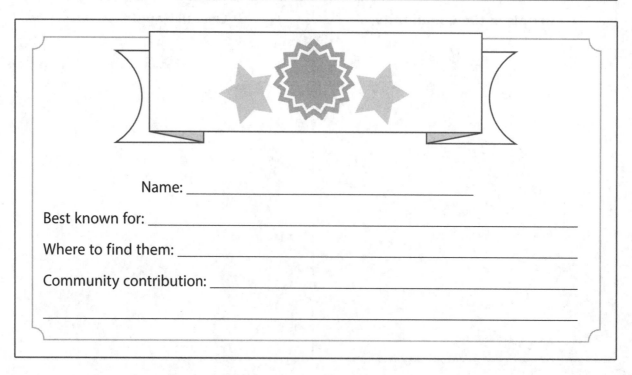

Name: _____

Best known for: _____

Where to find them: _____

Community contribution: _____

_____

Name: _____

Best known for: _____

Where to find them: _____

Community contribution: _____

_____

Name: _____ Date: _____

Developing Positive Relationships

Sometimes, it's hard to meet people who are not like us. Most people tend to spend most of their time with others who have similar backgrounds and interests. But meeting different kinds of people can make your life better! And it can make your community stronger and more unified.

Directions: Write how each person can make a connection with someone who is different from themself.

1. Phuong recently moved from Vietnam with his family. He speaks some English, but not much. Benji has noticed that Phuong sits alone during lunch. Benji has also noticed that Phuong likes the same comic books he does. How can Benji make a connection?

   _____

   _____

   _____

2. Kara lives down the hall from Mrs. Ellicott. Mrs. Ellicott is 93 years old and lives alone. Kara has noticed that she walks to the park every day around 4:00 and sits on the bench, feeding pigeons. How can Kara make a connection?

   _____

   _____

   _____

3. Gina's new neighbors just moved in. She hasn't met them yet, but she already knows that they have very different political views from Gina's family. The new neighbors immediately posted an election sign. Gina's not sure what to think of them. But she has seen their puppy out in the backyard. Gina has a two-month-old golden retriever who loves to play.

   _____

   _____

   _____

Focus on Community
Relationship Skills

Name: _____ Date: _____

Change Can Be Good

Change can be hard. But sometimes, change can lead to great things. Your community might try new ideas in order to make its services and opportunities better for the people who live there.

Directions: Imagine that your city or town has decided to build a new community center. What do you think it should be used for? Write a short letter to the editor explaining your reasons. Be specific.

Dear Editor,

_____

_____

_____

_____

_____

_____

_____

_____

_____

_____

_____

_____

_____

_____

_____

_____

_____

Sincerely,

_____

Focus on Community

Responsible Decision-Making

Name: _____ **Date:** _____

Cultures in Your State

Every state is a unique collection of cultures and people. Some cultural groups, such as American Indian tribes, are there because it is their traditional homeland. Some are there because their ancestors chose to settle there. Some are there because their ancestors were brought to this country against their will. All the different cultural groups enrich the current culture of your state.

Directions: Create a list of at least eight different cultural groups in your state. Be sure to include American Indian tribes that live in your area. Conduct research if needed. Then, draw your state. Include symbols that represent the groups you discovered.

_____   _____

_____   _____

_____   _____

_____   _____

Name:_____ Date:_____

Planning

Planning is a necessary skill. This is especially true while traveling. Planning can mean the difference between getting there and getting lost.

Focus on State

Self-Management

Directions: Imagine you are going on a statewide scavenger hunt. Locate each of the following places on a map of your state. Write their names. Then, draw the order in which you would want to visit them. Choose a route that is the most efficient and does not zigzag or backtrack.

A Trip around My State

State: _____

1. State capital: _____

2. The largest city (other than the capital): _____

3. The city or town farthest to the north: _____

4. The city or town farthest to the south: _____

5. The city or town farthest to the east: _____

6. The city or town farthest to the west: _____

Name: _____ Date: _____

Recognizing Others' Strengths

There are many essential workers we don't often think about. Grocery store clerks stock shelves with food. Mail carriers sort and deliver letters and packages. Bus drivers carry people to their destinations. All these people have strengths that make them good at their jobs.

Directions: List at least three traits that would be good strengths for people in each job to have. Use the character traits from the word bank, or write your own. Then, write two other essential jobs on the lines, and list their strengths.

Character Traits		
compassionate	honest	reliable
fair	intelligent	respectful
focused	leader	strong
good communicator	quick thinking	thoughtful

1. Grocery Store Clerks: _____

_____

2. Mail Carriers: _____

_____

3. Bus Drivers: _____

_____

4. Nurses: _____

_____

5. _____: _____

_____

6. _____: _____

_____

Focus on State

Social Awareness

Name:_____ Date:_____

Standing Up for Others

Part of being a responsible person is speaking up when something is wrong. Sometimes, that can seem difficult or even scary. One way to make it easier is to join with other people.

Directions: Read the text, and answer the questions about how you and others could stand up to injustice. Then, create a poster to get others involved.

Hurtful Message

There was a racist message discovered in your town this week. It was spray-painted onto a playground structure. This wasn't the first time something like this happened. Several towns and cities near yours have had similar things happen in the last few weeks. It seems to be happening more and more frequently.

1. What could you do by yourself?

_____

_____

2. What could you do with others?

_____

_____

Name: _____ Date: _____

Be Curious

Trying new things and going to new places is good for your mind and your mood. There are many amazing outdoor places to visit and explore that you may never have experienced or even heard about. Your own state is a great place to start exploring.

Directions: List two natural outdoor sites in your state that you've never visited. If you do not know where to start, search online. Write what you would do there and whom you would take with you. Then, draw yourself visiting one of the sites.

Place: _____

Activity: _____

Person: _____

Place: _____

Activity: _____

Person: _____

Responsible Decision-Making

Focus on State

Name: _____ Date: _____

Focus on Country

Self-Awareness

Personal and Social Identities

Part of your identity as an individual includes the country in which you live. You have your own ideas about what your country is like. But people in other countries may see it differently. Their views of your country could be based on movies or news stories they've seen. This can all cause them to have positive or negative impressions of your country.

Directions: Complete the Venn diagram with words and pictures. List your opinions and observations about your country. List things you think people from other countries might think about your country. Circle all the positive things, and underline all the negative things.

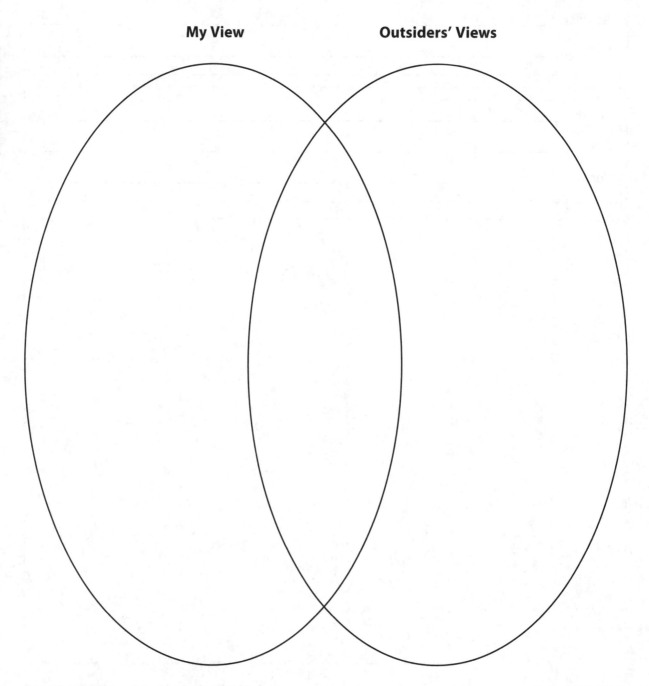

My View   **Outsiders' Views**

Name: _____ Date: _____

Setting Goals

It's important for individuals and groups to set goals. Goals provide direction and motivation to work hard and keep going. Goals also provide a way to measure progress and adjust plans.

Countries set goals, too. A goal of many countries is to use less fossil fuels. One option is to find more efficient sources of energy, such as solar power. Another option is for people to use less energy in their daily lives.

Directions: Brainstorm one specific thing you can do to use less energy in your daily life. Create a poster that encourages other people to do the same.

Name: _____ Date: _____

Focus on Country

Social Awareness

Empathy

Every time you stop to think about something from someone else's perspective, you are being empathetic. Having empathy means you are able to put yourself in someone else's shoes. It's not always easy to do. But it's an important skill. It will help you build strong relationships and help other people.

Directions: Read each scenario. Explain how each person can show empathy for their relatives in a difficult situation.

1. Laura is from Alabama, but her cousins live in California. They normally see each other every summer, but not this year. A mudslide damaged her cousins' apartment. They have to move out for a few weeks so that repairs can be made. They're staying in a motel while they wait.

   _____

   _____

   _____

   _____

2. Yousef's grandparents live in Michigan. They recently had a huge winter storm. It knocked down many trees in their neighborhood. One of them hit his grandparents' car. Nobody was hurt, but the car was totaled.

   _____

   _____

   _____

   _____

3. Dan's uncle lives in the state of Washington. Dan talks to him every week. This week, his uncle mentioned that the wildfire that's been raging for days is getting close to his home. He will have to evacuate, and he's not sure when he'll be allowed back.

   _____

   _____

   _____

   _____

   _____

Name: _____ Date: _____

Leadership

There are many leaders in our country. Some are easy to identify, such as politicians or military leaders. Some are a little less apparent. But all of them have a difficult job—to inspire, guide, and manage large groups of people.

Directions: Think of effective leaders you know, either in history or in your life. What characteristics make them effective? Fill the leader's head with as many characteristics as you can think of. Include both words and pictures.

Effective Leader

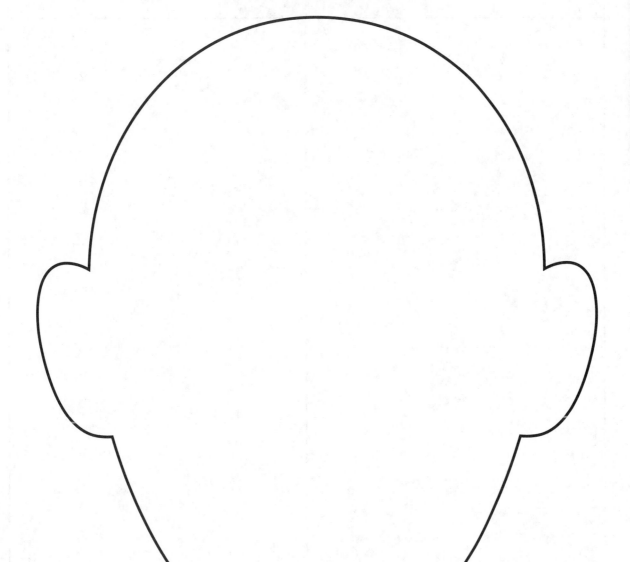

Name: _____ Date: _____

Making Good Decisions

It can be challenging to make big decisions. It's important to make sure you take time to think about them. Analyze all the information you have in order to make your decisions. This is true whether it's a personal decision or a political one.

Directions: Imagine your friend wants to run for president when they grow up. Consider the reasons for (pro) and against (con) your friend running for president. Create a pros and cons list with at least four reasons for each. Then, circle your three best reasons.

Pros	Cons

 126962—180 Days of Social-Emotional Learning

Name: _____ **Date:** _____

Identities That Unite Us

People around the world have many differences and unique qualities. They practice different religions. They speak different languages. They eat different foods and wear different clothes. But we all have a lot in common as well.

Directions: Think about the ways in which all people are similar. Complete the web to show what you have in common with other people in the world. Then, answer the question.

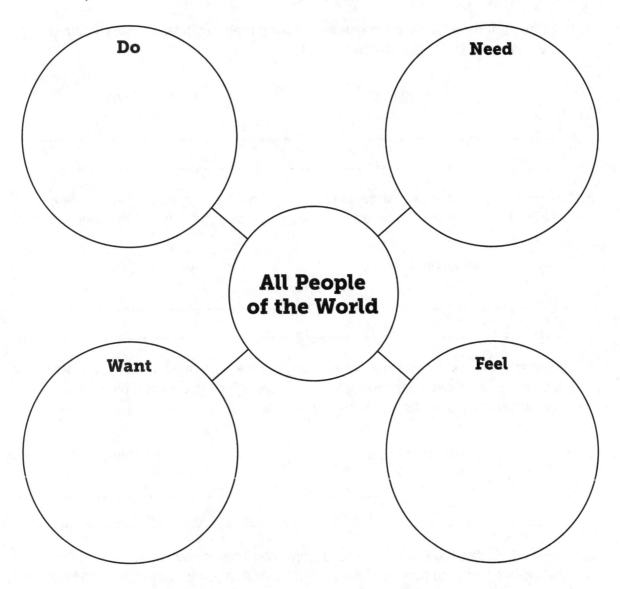

Do

Need

All People of the World

Want

Feel

1. Why might it be useful to think about all the things we have in common?

_____

_____

_____

Focus on World

Self-Awareness

Name: _____ Date: _____

Focus on World

Self-Management

You Can Help Take Care of the World

Everyone has problems. Cities, states, and countries have problems, too. There are even problems that require countries to work together in order to solve them. But even when there are global problems, individuals like you can still help.

Directions: Read each scenario. Circle whether it is a global or local problem. Then, write at least one action you could take to help.

1. Polar bears and penguins are in danger of losing their habitats. Global climate change is causing the polar ice caps to melt rapidly.

    global problem   local problem

    _____

    _____

2. The amount of trash on the streets in your town has been increasing lately. People leave trash by the side of the road. You have even seen trash left at the playground.

    global problem   local problem

    _____

    _____

3. The rates of depression and anxiety in young people have been rising in your area. You have friends who have been struggling, and several kids in the local high school have been hospitalized recently for mental health issues.

    global problem   local problem

    _____

    _____

4. Millions of people have been displaced from their homes and countries. These refugees are forced to flee from violence or other dangerous conditions. They live in temporary camps or in new countries, where they often don't know the language or culture.

    global problem   local problem

    _____

    _____

Name: _____ **Date:** _____

Gratitude

Everyone knows that it's nice to say thank you. But did you know that saying thank you can benefit you just as much as the person you thank? Expressing gratitude means telling why you appreciate or are thankful for someone or something. And every time you express gratitude, you reduce your stress levels and increase your own happiness. It's a win-win!

Directions: Think about someone who has made a difference in the world. It can be someone from today or from history. Write them a thank you note to express why you are grateful to them.

THANK YOU

Dear _____,

_____

_____

_____

_____

_____

_____

_____

_____

_____

_____

_____

_____

Sincerely,

_____

Name:_____ Date:_____

Cultural Competency

The world has many different cultures. Those differences can cause confusion. They can lead to misunderstandings. When you communicate with someone from another culture, it's OK to ask questions. Learn as much as you can. This can lead to *cultural competency*, or the ability to communicate well across cultures.

Focus on World

Relationship Skills

Directions: Identify the miscommunication in each scenario. Then, explain why it happened.

1. Jody and her family are visiting France on vacation. They're having a fantastic time exploring museums and sampling the local cuisine. But one night at dinner, Jody is horrified. The food arrives, and she gets a plate of beef that looks like it's raw. She is sure she had ordered a hamburger. She refuses to eat it or anything else that evening.

   _____
   _____
   _____
   _____

2. Liam's family invited their new neighbors to their home. The Amin family recently moved to the United States from Iraq. Liam's mom brought out a tray of cookies. Mr. Amin apologized and explained that they can't eat anything until after dusk. They are observing the holiday of Ramadan. Liam's mom did not know what that means, but she was a little offended that they wouldn't have just one cookie.

   _____
   _____
   _____
   _____

3. Chen is a foreign exchange student. One day at school, the teacher points at a few students and asks them to take something to the office for her. Chen is horrified. Pointing is very rude in his culture. He calls home to complain about how rude Americans are.

   _____
   _____
   _____
   _____

Identifying Solutions

Conflict happens all the time between people, families, or countries. There are different ways to solve conflicts. Under an authoritarian approach, one side makes a decision. There is no negotiation. Under a compromising approach, both sides try to make everyone somewhat happy. Everyone gives up some of what they want. And everyone gets some of what they want.

Directions: Read each conflict. Circle whether the approach is authoritarian or compromising. Then, answer the question.

1. Two countries share a border along a river. Both countries use it for drinking water. One country begins to use a portion of the river to dispose of waste from factories. When their neighbor complains, they refuse to listen or change their behavior.

    authoritarian   compromising

2. Three countries argue over control of a city. They all claim that it is part of their country's history. The leaders from each country meet. They decide to create an independent city that all three countries would help maintain.

    authoritarian   compromising

3. Until recently, no one paid much attention to a small island off the coast of many countries. Then, someone found that it has valuable minerals. One of the countries nearby claimed the island right away. They built a military outpost almost overnight. They are claiming full control of the island and its minerals.

    authoritarian   compromising

4. Which approach do you think is better? Why?

    _____

    _____

    _____

5. Is the other approach ever useful? Explain.

    _____

    _____

    _____

Responsible Decision-Making

Focus on World

Name:_____ Date:_____

Focus on Self

Self-Awareness

Identifying Emotions

Sometimes, it's easy to identify how you're feeling. Sometimes, it's a little trickier. You might know you're feeling something negative. But is it embarrassment? Is it nervousness? Is it anger? Is it fear? It can help to slow down and think about how your body is feeling.

Directions: Complete the charts as you think about times you felt embarrassed, nervous, and angry. First, write what happened to cause the emotion. Then, write the physical reaction that each emotion caused.

Cause	**Emotion**	**Physical Reaction**
_____ _____ _____	embarrassment	_____ _____ _____

Cause	**Emotion**	**Physical Reaction**
_____ _____ _____	nervousness	_____ _____ _____

Cause	**Emotion**	**Physical Reaction**
_____ _____ _____	anger	_____ _____ _____

Name: _____ **Date:** _____

Stress Management Strategies

One way to relieve stress or negative feelings is to do something you enjoy. It's a good idea to have a mental menu of fun options prepared, just in case you need them.

Directions: Think about all the things you do that make you happy. Maybe it's listening to your favorite song. Maybe it's eating your favorite snack. List as many as you can think of in each category.

Things I can create…

Things I can listen to…

Someone I can talk to…

Things I can do for other people…

Things I can do to relax…

Things I can do to be active…

Name:_____ Date:_____

Taking Others' Perspectives

When events happen that involve you, it's natural to focus on how they affect you. But other people are also affected. It's important to pay attention to how other people feel in a situation. Try imagining how you would feel if you were in another person's shoes. When in doubt, you can always ask.

Directions: Write how other people in each scenario might feel and why.

1. You win several academic awards at the end-of-year ceremony. Your best friend doesn't win anything. Your family takes both of you out for ice cream afterward. How might your friend feel?

   _____

   _____

   _____

2. Your soccer team wins the state championship. It was a great game, but you didn't get to play. You sat on the bench the entire time. The team goes out for dinner afterward, but you are feeling sorry for yourself. How does the rest of the team feel?

   _____

   _____

   _____

3. You failed the last history test. You studied for it, so you were not expecting to fail. It's the first bad grade you've ever gotten in that class. Your teacher calls you over and offers you the chance to take a retest next week. You mumble an answer and walk out of the classroom. How does your teacher feel?

   _____

   _____

   _____

4. You just got the new game you have been asking for. You are thrilled and talk about how great it is all day. Your friend is not allowed to play this game. How does your friend feel?

   _____

   _____

   _____

Name: _____ **Date:** _____

Nonverbal Communication

We often focus on people's words when we are communicating. These verbal messages certainly have a lot of meaning. But our bodies can "say" a lot as well. This nonverbal communication is a powerful tool. You can tell a lot about how someone is feeling or what they are thinking based on nonverbal cues.

Directions: Read each scenario. Explain how the person is feeling and which nonverbal cues tell you this.

1. Jayden sits down after finishing his oral presentation. His eyes are scrunched together. He sighs loudly and puts his head down on the desk. You tell him, "Good job!" He looks up for a moment and shrugs. "Thanks," he says quietly.

   _____

   _____

   _____

   _____

2. "What is with you today?" you ask your friend, Cece. "Nothing," she says with a sharp tone. "I'm fine." She rolls her eyes and turns her back away from you. "Did I do something wrong?" you ask. She spins around and just looks at you. Then, she turns her back to you and storms off down the hallway.

   _____

   _____

   _____

   _____

3. Two of your best friends are standing under a tree. You have just come back outside after running inside to grab some water. The two of them see you and smile. Then, they lean close to each other and whisper. They look back at you again and shout, "Hurry up already!" You run over, and they give you a high five.

   _____

   _____

   _____

   _____

Relationship Skills

Focus on Self

Name: _____ Date: _____

Focus on Self

Responsible Decision-Making

Resisting Peer Pressure

Peer pressure is when people your age (your peers) try to convince you to do something. Sometimes, it's obvious. They might tell you that all the cool people do it. Sometimes, it's more subtle. They might exclude people who don't go along with the crowd. It's a good idea to have a plan in case you find yourself in a situation where you don't want to bend to peer pressure.

Directions: Draw a line to match each scenario to a response that would help you avoid peer pressure. Responses may be used more than once. Or you can write your own.

Scenarios

Responses

You're the only one of your friends who isn't on social media. You don't really want to join, but your friends keep telling you you're missing out.

Use humor. Make a joke about how much you follow the rules, and you just can't help it.

The student next to you is playing a video game during class and asks you to join them. You don't want to get in trouble in school, but they laugh at you when you say no.

Tell them that's not cool. You're too smart for that.

Say, "No thanks," and leave.

You're at the park with some friends. One of them dares you to stick your tongue to a frozen pole. You know it would get stuck and cause a lot of pain.

Tell them that they can do whatever they want, but you'll say no for now.

You need to study for a test, but your friend tells you to blow it off. They say you could look at another person's paper.

_____
_____
_____

Name: _____ **Date:** _____

Honesty and Integrity

Being a good friend means being someone who is honest and trustworthy. Honesty means always telling the whole truth, even when it's difficult. Being trustworthy means that other people can always count on you to keep your word. A person who can be trusted to keep their word has integrity. These are all qualities of a good friend.

Directions: Read the story. Then, answer the questions.

Friday Night Choice

Elena and Sophie are best friends. They've known each other since kindergarten. Their families even vacation together. This weekend is the opening of a new movie starring their favorite actor. They've been looking forward to this weekend for a long time. Elena and Sophie were planning to go on Friday night, right after dinner. But on Friday morning, one of their other friends invites Elena to a slumber party at her house that night. Elena doesn't want to miss the party, but she made a promise to Sophie. She isn't sure what to do.

1. What is the problem?

   _____

   _____

2. What would Elena do if she focused only on herself? How would she feel about herself?

   _____

   _____

   _____

3. What would Elena do if she acted with integrity? How would she feel about herself?

   _____

   _____

   _____

4. What do you think Elena should choose? Why?

   _____

   _____

   _____

Focus on Friends

Self-Awareness

Name: _____ Date: _____

Recognizing Others' Strengths

Your friends are your friends for a reason. There is something about each of them that you appreciate and makes them special. We don't often stop to think about all the wonderful qualities that our friends have.

Directions: Complete the ID badges about two of your friends.

I.D.   **BADGE #00**

Name: _____

Strongest abilities: _____

Makes me laugh when: _____

I can count on them to: _____

Key personality traits: _____

My favorite thing to do with them: _____

I.D.   **BADGE #00**

Name: _____

Strongest abilities: _____

Makes me laugh when: _____

I can count on them to: _____

Key personality traits: _____

My favorite thing to do with them: _____

Name: _____ Date: _____

Empathy

Empathizing with others means you are able to understand how they feel, even if you have never had the same experience. You might think of it as putting yourself in their shoes. Empathy is often what people really want when they're feeling down. They need someone to understand and acknowledge how they feel. They want to feel less alone.

Directions: Read each scenario. Write both a verbal and nonverbal way to show empathy for each person's feelings.

1. Your friend, David, storms in and slams his backpack down on his desk. He starts to tell you about how his younger sister ruined one of the presents he just received for his birthday. He hadn't even gotten to play with it yet.

   Verbal: _____

   _____

   Nonverbal: _____

   _____

2. You're in the cafeteria, and you see your friend Jasmine. You wave her over to your table. As she approaches, she trips and her food goes flying everywhere. She's covered in spaghetti and looks like she's about to cry.

   Verbal: _____

   _____

   Nonverbal: _____

   _____

3. Your best friend, Tanya, tried out for the basketball team. She made it to the second day of tryouts on Tuesday. But when you both arrived at school on Wednesday, her name was not on the list. She was surprised and really upset.

   Verbal: _____

   _____

   Nonverbal: _____

   _____

Focus on Friends

Social Awareness

Name: _____ Date: _____

Communicating Effectively

Have you ever played the telephone game? It starts on one end with a simple message. Then, it passes from person to person. By the time it gets to the end, the message is usually completely different. In real life, this happens all the time. If you rely on someone else to tell you what someone said, you're likely to get an inaccurate message. These mix-ups can lead to confusion and hurt feelings.

Directions: Read each scenario, and answer the questions.

1. Someone stole the field trip money from the science classroom yesterday. The teacher announced that the trip will be canceled unless they can find the money. Max tells Isaac that their friend Sam took it and hid it. What could Isaac do to find out more about what happened?

   _____

   _____

   _____

   _____

2. Maggie overhears two of her friends talking about their plans for the weekend. They're going to play paintball. She's been dying to go, and she has talked about it with both of them in the past. She can't understand why they didn't ask her. What could Maggie say to her friends to avoid a miscommunication?

   _____

   _____

   _____

   _____

3. Tyler notices two of his friends whispering. When he gets closer, he hears them say that their other friend, Jen, got in big trouble with her parents last night. How should Tyler find out more about what happened?

   _____

   _____

   _____

   _____

Name: _____ Date: _____

Making Decisions

Decision-making can be hard. It can be even harder when you're trying to make a decision with friends. It's hard to separate what you think from what your friends think. It can help to think about the interests of each person or group involved.

Directions: Read the story. Write what is best for Lucas, his friends, and the group as a whole. Then, answer the question.

Group Project

Lucas and two of his friends are working on a group project. They have to create a presentation on a country of their choice. Lucas wants to do Argentina. His family is from Argentina, so he has lots of items they can use for the presentation. Plus, they can ask his parents lots of questions. They could even make some Argentinian food. Lucas's friends both want to do Italy. They love Italian food and want to make pizza for the class.

Best for Lucas

Best for His Friends

Best for the Group

1. What do you think they should do? Why?

_____

_____

_____

Name:_____ Date:_____

Focus on Community

Self-Awareness

Examining Prejudice

Sometimes, adults have ideas about young people and how they behave. These fixed ideas might even be prejudices. A prejudice is an opinion that someone has about a person or group that is not based on fact. Prejudices can be harmful. But they can also be changed if people are open to new information or experiences.

Directions: Answer the questions.

1. What do the adults in your community think about people your age? How do you know?

_____

_____

_____

2. Why do you think adults tend to think this way about people your age?

_____

_____

_____

3. Imagine an adult had a negative view about people your age. What information could you share to make them think differently?

_____

_____

_____

4. How might different experiences, performances, or events help someone overcome a prejudice they have?

_____

_____

_____

126962—180 Days of Social-Emotional Learning

© Shell Education

Name: _____ **Date:** _____

Being Accountable

To be accountable for something means that you are responsible for it. We can all be accountable for our own communities. This doesn't mean you need to do everything. But part of being accountable means that you help your community when you can.

Directions: Read each scenario. Write one thing that the people could do to improve their communities.

1. Chloe and Alyssa were walking down the street to the park. They were disgusted to see that someone had left a bunch of litter on the side of the road. It was right next to a preschool, too!

   _____

   _____

   _____

2. Aiden and Matt want to play basketball. But the hoop is broken on both ends of the court in their neighborhood. There's no basket, and the backboard is cracked. The fence around the court is old and falling apart, too.

   _____

   _____

   _____

3. Josh and Emily live next door to an elderly woman named Rose. Rose lives alone and uses a walker to get around. She's always nice to the kids and loves to see them play in the neighborhood. Last night, there was a huge snowstorm. Josh and Emily went sledding all day. On their way home, they noticed that Rose's walkway and stairs are still covered in snow and ice.

   _____

   _____

   _____

Focus on Community

Self-Management

Name: _____ Date: _____

Focus on Community

Social Awareness

New in Town

Think about a community you know very well. It might be where you live now. Or it might be another place you have lived in the past or one you have visited often. You probably know a lot about that community. But someone who has just moved there will not. It can be tough to navigate a new city or town. Advice and information from other residents can be extremely helpful.

Directions: Create a welcome flyer that would help someone your age who is new to your community. Include the categories below and at least one of your own. Add information and pictures or maps to your design.

Categories

parks	school
places to have fun	stores

Community Pride

Strong communities often have strong identities. People know what the community stands for. They are proud to be part of it. Communities can encourage these feelings through things such as events, slogans, and symbols.

Directions: Imagine that your community has decided to paint a mural in the center of town to show the good things about your community. Draw your design for the mural. Consider showing realistic images of your community as well as symbols. Use color to make it stand out. Then, explain why you included the elements you chose.

Focus on Community

Relationship Skills

_____

_____

_____

Name: _____ Date: _____

Evaluating Community Impacts

Many communities have some outdoor spaces where people can enjoy nature. There might be forests where you can hike or parks with a few trees and a basketball court. Whatever the outdoor spaces include, they are all assets to their communities.

Directions: A community is building a new park. Community leaders are asking for input about three possible locations. They are holding a public forum to hear from people. Write a speech about where you think the park should go and why.

Location 1: Five acres of land right next to a lake. Part of the lake would be blocked off for public use.

Location 2: A 20-acre forest at the edge of town that could be purchased with public money. Part of the forest would be cleared, but most of it would remain forest.

Location 3: Five acres of flat space in the middle of town.

_____

_____

_____

_____

_____

_____

_____

_____

_____

_____

_____

_____

_____

_____

_____

_____

_____

Name: _____ **Date:** _____

State Assets

Your state has many assets. Assets are strengths, resources, or positive characteristics. They help make a person or place unique. Your state's assets include its people and cultures. It also includes its places, events, or natural resources.

Directions: Write an acrostic poem about your state. An acrostic poem is one in which the first letter of each line spells a word. In this case, that word is your state's name. Include some of your state's assets in your poem.

State Name: _____

_____ _____

_____ _____

_____ _____

_____ _____

_____ _____

_____ _____

_____ _____

_____ _____

_____ _____

_____ _____

_____ _____

_____ _____

Focus on State

Self-Awareness

Name: _____ Date: _____

Focus on State

Self-Management

Goals and Milestones

People often set individual goals. They might decide to train for a marathon or learn how to play the piano. States can set goals, too. In order for any person or government to reach any big goal, it's helpful to set milestones. Milestones are smaller deadlines along the way to a bigger goal. They help track progress so you don't fall behind.

Directions: Imagine a state set a goal to reduce energy use during the summer by 20 percent. Write two smaller goals the state could set to support their larger goal of reducing energy use. Then, draw a picture to inspire people to reduce their energy use.

1. _____

   _____

2. _____

   _____

Name: _____ Date: _____

Focus on State

Social Awareness

The Influences of Organizations

Each state government makes its own laws for the people who live there. These may vary from state to state. One example of rules that are different are those that dictate how old children must be before they can legally be left home alone. Each state is different. Some states have no regulations about this issue.

Directions: Study the data in the table, and then answer the questions.

State	Minimum Age to Leave a Child Alone
Kansas	6 (recommended, not required)
Maryland	8
Illinois	14 (for a reasonable amount of time)

1. Why do you think these rules vary so much?

_____

_____

2. What do you think the minimum age should be in your state? Explain.

_____

_____

_____

3. Do you think the age should be the same everywhere? Explain.

_____

_____

_____

4. How might these laws affect families living in these states?

_____

_____

_____

Name: _____ Date: _____

Developing Positive Relationships

Laughter is an extremely powerful tool. It can make you feel better. It can also help resolve conflicts and build relationships between people. Laughter can provide a healthy perspective on your life.

Directions: Find a partner, and complete this silly story about your state together. Ask your partner for each type of word, and record their answers on the lines. Be sure not to read the story until you have completed all of it. Then, read the finished story aloud.

_____ is best known for its _____.
(name of your state)   *(plural noun)*

They can be found on nearly every corner. People line up for hours just

to _____ them! Not many people know that these
   (verb)

_____ _____ can easily be found on any
(adjective)   *(plural noun)*

_____ in the state! It just takes a little bit of work and
(location)

about _____.
      (amount of time)

Most people like to _____ them. But true locals know
                     (verb)

that you really want to _____ them with _____.
                        (verb)   *(noun)*

Mmmm, delicious! At _____, many people like to
                    (name of holiday)

_____ them with _____ and _____.
(verb)   *(noun)*   *(noun)*

What could be better?

Focus on State

Relationship Skills

© Shell Education

Anticipating and Evaluating Consequences

Every choice has consequences. When the people who run your state make choices or set goals, those choices have consequences. There is usually some kind of benefit and some kind of tradeoff. That means you have to give something up to get another thing that you want. If the state chooses to spend money in one area, for example, it will have less to spend in another.

Directions: Describe the potential benefits and tradeoffs of the choices made by each state. In your responses, consider how that choice could affect the people who live there.

1. A state decides to host a large international sporting event. That means they will have to build several large stadiums. They will also have to improve the public transportation system around the capital city. Spectators will need a way to get to the events easily. They will also need enough places to sleep and plenty of places to eat.

   _____
   _____
   _____
   _____

2. A state is considering building a new bullet train system to connect its two largest cities. They will have to help pay for the construction of the train and tracks.

   _____
   _____
   _____
   _____

3. A state wants to change its high school graduation requirements. The new rules would require every student to take four years of a foreign language in high school. Local high schools complain that their students already have a lot of classes. Students have a hard time fitting everything into their schedules.

   _____
   _____
   _____
   _____
   _____

Focus on State

Responsible Decision-Making

Name: _____ Date: _____

Focus on Country

Self-Awareness

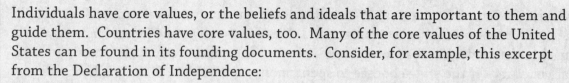

Core Values

Individuals have core values, or the beliefs and ideals that are important to them and guide them. Countries have core values, too. Many of the core values of the United States can be found in its founding documents. Consider, for example, this excerpt from the Declaration of Independence:

"We hold these truths to be self-evident, that all men are created equal, that they are endowed by their Creator with certain unalienable Rights, that among these are Life, Liberty and the pursuit of Happiness."

Directions: Complete the web to describe three core values of the United States from the Declaration of Independence. Add three more American core values you have seen or experienced.

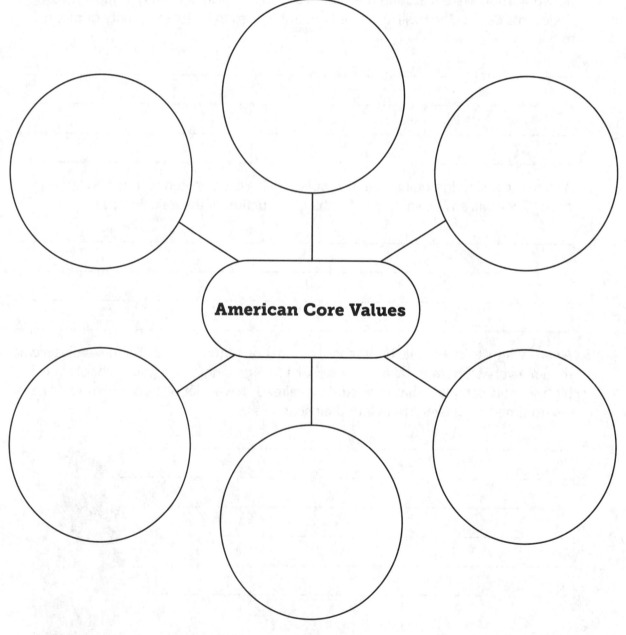

American Core Values

Name: _____ Date: _____

Using Planning and Organizational Skills

As you get older, you will have more things to do and more places to go. Sometimes, these events will be required, but other times you will be able to choose what you do. This means you will need to prioritize your schedule to determine what you want to do.

Directions: Choose one holiday that you would like to celebrate. Describe why you would like to celebrate it, and then draw your celebration.

National Cake Day	Say Hello Day
National Flossing Day	Square Dancing Day
Electronic Greetings Day	National Red Mitten Day
Celebrate Your Unique Talent Day	National Sardines Day

Focus on Country

Self-Management

Name: _____ Date: _____

Taking Others' Perspectives

Solving big and small problems means you need to understand all sides of the story. You must be able to see things from other perspectives.

Directions: Read the story, and complete the speech bubbles to show the perspectives of both sides. Then, answer the question.

Toll Road Dilemma

The towns of Gilbertsville and Haughton are just five miles apart, but they are in different states. Recently, a new mall was built in Haughton, so people from Gilbertsville frequently cross the border to Haughton. They shop, eat at restaurants, and go to the movies. With all this travel, there is much more traffic than before. The roads are wearing down, and trash is piling up. Haughton residents want to install a toll booth so people from Gilbertsville have to pay to come to their town. The state would use the money from the tolls to fix the roads and clean up trash, but it could cause a conflict with their neighboring state.

Gilbertsville   **Haughton**

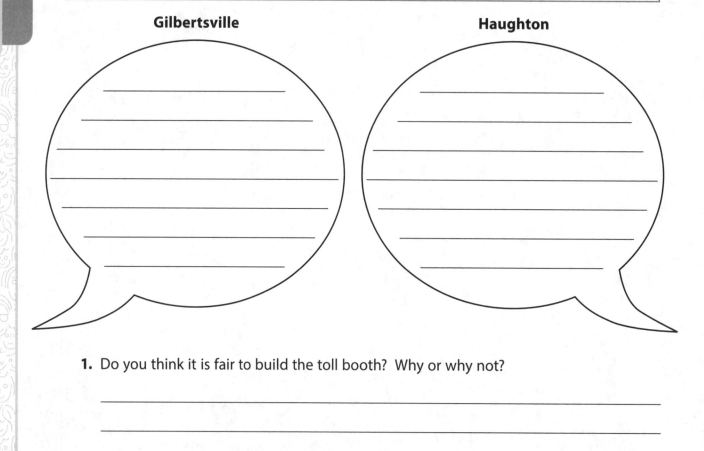

1. Do you think it is fair to build the toll booth? Why or why not?

_____

_____

_____

_____

Name: _____ Date: _____

Standing Up for What Is Right

Many people in the history of the United States have stood up for what is fair and right. They stood up for civil rights, freedom from slavery, and women's rights, among others. It was not always easy, and they often faced angry people who opposed them. Sometimes, they were arrested or attacked. But all of them were brave enough to decide that the right thing to do was more important than their fear.

Directions: Imagine you could host a dinner party with a courageous leader from the past or present. Choose a person from the list, or come up with your own. Write at least two questions you would ask that person. Write what their responses might be.

Example Leaders

Sojourner Truth	Francisco P. Ramirez	John Lewis
Abraham Lincoln	Martin Luther King Jr.	Susan B. Anthony
Helen Keller	Ruby Bridges	Tammy Duckworth

My Dinner Guest: _____

1. Question

_____

_____

_____

2. Response

_____

_____

_____

3. Question

_____

_____

_____

4. Response

_____

_____

_____

Focus on Country

Relationship Skills

Name:_____ Date:_____

Identifying Solutions

The United States is a very large country. Each state has its own problems and priorities. The government has to juggle all these issues and projects in order to make decisions that benefit as many people as possible. They have to decide how to spend money and what to do first.

Directions: Circle whether you think each situation is an urgent problem or if it can wait. Explain each answer. Then, place them in order of priority, from first (1) to last (4).

_____ 1. The Natural Disaster Preparation Plan document has not been updated in five years.

        urgent problem   can wait

_____

_____

_____ 2. A river has become polluted. It provides drinking water for four states.

        urgent problem   can wait

_____

_____

_____ 3. There is an economic depression. Nearly 40 percent of all Americans are unemployed.

        urgent problem   can wait

_____

_____

_____ 4. The national highway system needs to be upgraded. At least 15 percent of all bridges and overpasses need immediate repair.

        urgent problem   can wait

_____

_____

Name:_____ Date:_____

Developing Interests

Our world has an amazing variety of countries. Unfortunately, it is expensive and time-consuming to visit all of them. But you can explore elements of other countries from home. One way to do that is by sampling food from other places.

Directions: Select a country that you do not already know much about. Research the food of that country. Answer the questions to record your findings.

Country: _____

1. What are some characteristics of the traditional food in this country?

_____

_____

_____

2. Record a recipe from this country:

_____

_____

_____

_____

_____

_____

_____

_____

_____

_____

_____

3. Would you sample this recipe? Why or why not?

_____

_____

_____

Focus on World

Self-Awareness

Name: _____   Date: _____

SMART Goals

In order to accomplish a long list of priorities, countries must set goals and make plans. Effective goals are SMART. *S* stands for *specific* because a good goal states exactly what it will do. *M* stands for *measurable*, meaning someone can easily tell whether they have achieved the goal. *A* is for *achievable*, which means it must be realistic. *R* is for *relevant*, which means it should be a goal that matters. *T* is for *timely*, because a goal with a deadline is more likely to be reached.

Directions: Choose one thing you would change to make the world a better place. Set a SMART goal that a world leader could use to achieve it. Then, answer the questions.

Goal: _____

1. How is the goal **specific**?

   _____

   _____

2. How is it **measurable**?

   _____

   _____

3. How is it **achievable**?

   _____

   _____

4. How is it **relevant**?

   _____

   _____

5. How is it **timely**?

   _____

   _____

Name: _____ Date: _____

Identifying Diverse Social Norms

Every country or culture has its own social norms. Norms are unwritten rules for how to behave. For example, in the United States, people generally tip their servers after eating in restaurants. It's not a law or a rule. But people expect you to do it. Other countries do things differently.

Directions: Imagine you have a pen pal from another country. Write them a letter to ask about social norms in their country. Include questions such as how to greet people, whether to talk about personal things (such as money and age), and how children speak to their elders. Be sure to explain your own norms as well.

Focus on World

Social Awareness

Name: _____ Date: _____

Resolving Conflicts Constructively

Sometimes, conflicts can be resolved in a way that makes everyone happy. Those solutions are called win-win. Everyone wins. Sometimes, conflicts end with only one side winning. Those solutions are called win-lose. Sometimes, no one is happy. Those solutions are called lose-lose.

Directions: Write how to resolve each international conflict with a win-win, win-lose, or lose-lose solution. Then, answer the question.

1. Two countries both want access to a large river for drinking water. What is a win-win solution to this problem?

   _____

   _____

   _____

2. Two countries fight over who gets access to limited oil resources. What is a win-lose solution to this problem?

   _____

   _____

   _____

3. Three countries use a bay for fishing. Right now, too many fish are being harvested, and the population will run out. What is a lose-lose solution to this problem?

   _____

   _____

   _____

4. Is a win-win solution always possible? Why or why not?

   _____

   _____

   _____

Name: _____ Date: _____

Causes and Effects of Conflicts

Sometimes, conflicts between countries are small. Other times, those conflicts can become violent and even escalate to a war. But every conflict can be traced back to an event or events that caused it. And every conflict has lasting effects.

Directions: Draw a line from each cause to its effect. Then, answer the questions.

Causes

Two countries both claim the same city as their own.

Multiple countries want control over unclaimed islands that have a lot of valuable resources.

One country's navy accidentally sinks an innocent fishing boat from another country.

Thousands of refugees from one country have flooded into another country.

Effects

Failed negotiations lead to war.

Other countries offer support and help build temporary shelters.

An uninvolved country hosts negotiations to find a way to share resources.

An apology is offered and accepted quickly. Money is sent in compensation.

1. What kinds of responses led to positive outcomes?

_____

_____

2. What kinds of responses led to negative outcomes?

_____

_____

Responsible Decision-Making

Focus on World

Name:_____ Date:_____

How Others See You

The way you see yourself may be different from how others see you. Other people can only judge by what they see you do and hear you say, but you know much more about your own thoughts and feelings.

Directions: Fill the person on the left with words or pictures to describe how you see yourself. Fill the person on the right with words or pictures to describe how others see you. Then, answer the question.

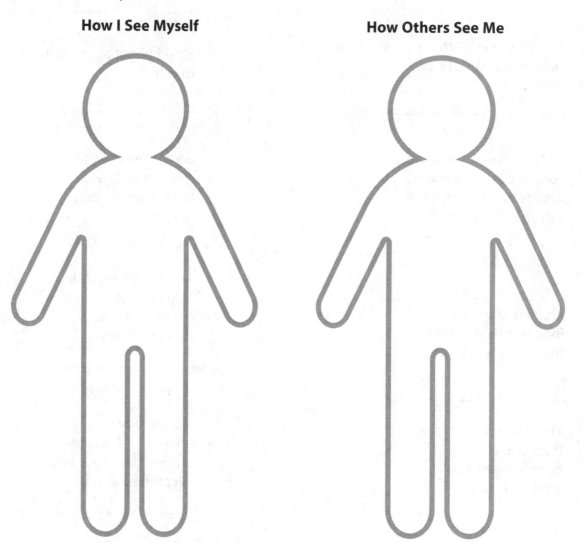

How I See Myself   **How Others See Me**

1. How different are the two versions of you? Explain why this might be.

_____

_____

_____

_____

Focus on Self
Self-Awareness

Name: _____ Date: _____

Managing Stress

Have you ever heard the phrase, "Laughter is the best medicine"? While it may not literally be true, laughter can have a powerful effect on your mood and your stress level. Sharing a joke with a friend can be a great way to lift your spirits.

Directions: Write three of your favorite jokes in the speech bubbles. Make sure they are school appropriate. Then, tell them to your classmates. Put a star by the one that gets the biggest laugh.

Focus on Self — Self-Management

Name: _____ Date: _____

Understanding Gratitude

How do you feel when someone does something really nice for you? How do you feel when someone gives you a compliment? You probably feel very pleased, but you might also feel a little awkward. It can be hard to know how to show gratitude when someone does or says something nice. It can help to have a few phrases handy for when these situations arise.

Directions: For each situation, write a phrase you could say in response. Choose one of the sample phrases, or write your own.

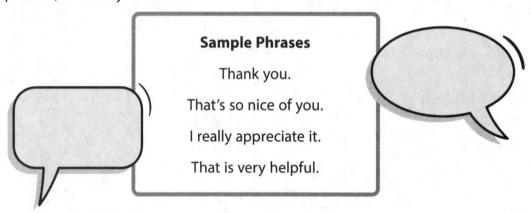

Sample Phrases

Thank you.

That's so nice of you.

I really appreciate it.

That is very helpful.

1. A classmate tells you they like your new shoes.

   _____

2. Someone holds the door open for you while you are carrying a bag of groceries.

   _____

3. A teacher compliments you on your solo performance.

   _____

4. A classmate lends you a pencil for a quiz.

   _____

Directions: Answer the questions.

5. How do you feel when someone compliments you?

   _____

   _____

6. How do you feel when someone thanks you?

   _____

   _____

Name:_____ Date:_____

Resolving Conflicts

Everybody makes mistakes. Unfortunately, those mistakes can cause problems for other people. It's usually a good idea to apologize quickly when you realize you've made a mistake. Then, you can offer to help make up for any damage you may have caused. The longer you wait, the harder it gets to make things better.

Focus on Self

Relationship Skills

Directions: Answer the questions.

1. Describe a time you made a mistake and apologized. Include what the mistake was, how you apologized, and how you felt afterward.

   _____

   _____

   _____

   _____

2. Describe a time you made a mistake but did not apologize. Include what happened and how you felt afterward.

   _____

   _____

   _____

   _____

3. Do you wish you had apologized for the situation in question 2? Why or why not?

   _____

   _____

   _____

4. Describe a time someone apologized to you. Include what happened and how you felt before and after the apology.

   _____

   _____

   _____

   _____

Name: _____ Date: _____

Focus on Self

Responsible Decision-Making

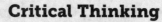

Critical Thinking

Sometimes, decisions need to be made quickly. When you make a decision quickly, you are more likely to overlook information that might be important. Pause and consider what the consequences might be before you make a choice.

Directions: Read the story, and answer the questions.

Baseball Decision

Leon and his friend Eric are hanging out at the park near Leon's house. Eric wants to play baseball at the field nearby. An adult and a few other kids are standing near the baseball diamond with bats, baseballs, and gloves. Eric suggests that Leon text the rest of their friends and tell them to come over to play baseball with them. Leon thinks the idea sounds like a lot of fun.

1. What is Leon's first reaction to Eric's suggestion?

   _____

   _____

2. If Leon were to pause to think about it, what might he say to Eric?

   _____

   _____

3. What questions could Leon ask himself?

   _____

   _____

4. How might Leon and Eric's decisions affect other people?

   _____

   _____

   _____

   _____

Name:_____ Date:_____

Knowing Your Strengths and Weaknesses

Every student has strengths and weaknesses. Learning involves many different skills, including being aware of those strengths and weaknesses. Everyone can work on their skills and improve as needed. It's good to know what you need to focus on in order to improve.

Focus on School

Self-Awareness

Directions: Study the list of skills. Put a plus sign next to your strengths. Put a star next to skills you need to work on. Underline skills you're not sure about. Then, answer the questions.

asking questions	calculating

drawing	experimenting

focusing	keeping track of time

leading a group	listening

making music	memorizing facts

moving quickly	painting

public speaking	reading

solving puzzles	using maps

writing stories

1. Which of the skills that you put a plus sign next to are you most proud of? Why?

_____

_____

_____

2. Which of the skills that you starred will help you the most? Why?

_____

_____

_____

Name:_____ Date:_____

Time Management

Students have to juggle many different assignments with different due dates. It's important to have an organized way to keep track of all your schoolwork. It's also important to estimate how long each task will take you. Otherwise, you might run out of time.

Directions: Imagine you have been assigned all the tasks below. Write how long you think each task will take. Then, write the tasks in the planner. Make sure to give yourself enough time to get everything done. You may choose to spread some assignments out over multiple days.

1. A social studies project is due on Friday. You must read two articles and create a poster highlighting the key information.

_____

2. You have a math test on Tuesday and need to complete a 20-problem study guide.

_____

3. You have 30 pages left in a novel that you need to read for language arts by Wednesday.

_____

4. An art project is due Friday. You need to draw and color an eight-panel comic strip.

_____

5. You need to read a chapter in your science textbook and answer 10 questions by Thursday.

_____

Monday	Tuesday	Wednesday	Thursday
3 hours available	3 hours available	2 hours available	1 hour available

© Shell Education

Name: _____ Date: _____

Understanding the Influence of Organizations

You may have noticed that you behave differently with your friends from how you do with adults. There are different expectations and social norms in different places and with different people. It might be okay to interrupt your friends, for example. But your teacher might not be too happy about it.

Directions: List things you do when you're with friends that you would not do at school with teachers. List things you do at school with teachers that you would not do with your friends. Then, answer the question.

With Friends

With Teachers

1. What might happen if you did the things from the first box at school?

_____

_____

_____

Focus on School
Social Awareness

Name: _____ Date: _____

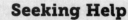

Focus on School

Relationship Skills

> ### Seeking Help
>
> Even the best students get confused or have questions when they are learning something new. But it can be hard to ask for help. You might worry that a teacher will think you're not paying attention. A teacher's reaction often depends on how you ask your question. It is important to show you're trying, ask something specific, and be polite.

Directions: Read each way a student asks for help, and answer the questions.

1. "Wait, what? Stop! What did you say? I'm totally lost."

   Did they show they're trying? _____

   Did they ask a specific question? _____

   Did they speak politely? _____

   How do you think the teacher will react to this request for help? Why?

   _____

   _____

2. "Can you please help me? I've been working on these fractions. The denominators are different, so I can't figure out what to do. Can you remind me what the next step is?"

   Did they show they're trying? _____

   Did they ask a specific question? _____

   Did they speak politely? _____

   How do you think the teacher will react to this request for help? Why?

   _____

   _____

3. "Can I ask a question, please? I found an example of rhyming in the poem. But I can't find any similes or metaphors. Could you give me an example of a simile?"

   Did they show they're trying? _____

   Did they ask a specific question? _____

   Did they speak politely? _____

   How do you think the teacher will react to this request for help? Why?

   _____

   _____

Name: _____ **Date:** _____

Trying New Things

School is a great place to explore new things, from clubs and student government to sports and activities. Consider trying something new every year. It can be a great way to discover new interests and make new friends.

Directions: Write two extracurricular activities at your school that you would like to try. Answer the questions about each one.

Name of Activity: _____

Why do you want to try this activity?

_____

_____

Why haven't you tried it yet?

_____

_____

Make a plan to try this new activity.

_____

_____

Name of Activity: _____

Why do you want to try this activity?

_____

_____

Why haven't you tried it yet?

_____

_____

Make a plan to try this new activity.

_____

_____

Responsible Decision-Making

Focus on School

Name: _____ Date: _____

Developing Interests and a Sense of Purpose

Every member of a community can find ways to help. You can volunteer for a local charity or other organization. You can also find ways to speak up about the things that matter to you.

Directions: You read a posting for a new Youth Advisory Board in your community. This group will represent young people's interests at community meetings. Write a letter explaining why you would be a good choice for this new board.

Focus on Community

Self-Awareness

To Whom it May Concern,

_____

_____

_____

_____

_____

_____

_____

_____

_____

_____

_____

_____

_____

_____

_____

_____

Sincerely,

_____

Name: _____ Date: _____

Managing Emotions

Managing your own emotions can be tricky. Trying to help other people manage strong emotions is even harder. But helping other people learn self-management techniques can help prevent problems. It can make you feel good, too, both now and when problems arise later.

Directions: Older kids in your community have recently been caught fighting. Adult leaders want to offer training or classes at school to help stop the violent behavior. Explain whether each option listed below would be effective and why. Then, suggest your own activity, and write a plan that incorporates at least two of these suggestions.

1. Yoga class _____
   _____

2. Mediation training _____
   _____

3. Communication class _____
   _____

4. Martial arts training _____
   _____

5. Book club _____
   _____

6. Your activity: _____
   _____

7. Your plan: _____
   _____
   _____
   _____
   _____
   _____

Focus on Community
Self-Management

Name:_____ Date:_____

Focus on Community

Social Awareness

Empathy and Compassion

People will not always agree about how to solve community problems. The same problems affect different groups in different ways. Even the solutions affect people in different ways. Think about all the perspectives when you try to solve a problem.

Directions: Read the story. Write how each group may have felt as they listened at the meeting. Explain why they may have felt that way.

To Build or Not to Build?

Your community held a public meeting to discuss whether it should raise taxes to build a new high school. There were many speakers on both sides. Some discussed the terrible condition of the current high school. Others discussed test scores and thought resources should be spent on academics before building a new school.

1. Teachers

_____

_____

_____

2. High school students

_____

_____

_____

3. Parents

_____

_____

_____

4. Community members without children

_____

_____

_____

Name: _____ Date: _____

Apologizing

It's important to apologize when you have done something wrong. All apologies need to be specific. Good apologies do not make excuses. They take responsibility for what has happened. They are also honest.

Directions: Write whether each statement is a good apology and why.

1. "Even though I did nothing wrong, I am sorry that the funds for the new school are no longer available."

   _____

   _____

2. "I'm sorry that I hit that man, but he provoked me."

   _____

   _____

3. "I'm sorry that the event was so crowded. It was my fault. We weren't prepared. I understand why everyone is upset."

   _____

   _____

4. I'm sorry I didn't turn my project in on time. I just had so much going on, and I couldn't find anyone who could help me.

   _____

   _____

5. I'm sorry I was late. I should have planned my time better.

   _____

   _____

Directions: Imagine your friend lets you borrow their game, and then you lose it. Write an apology to them. Remember to take responsibility and to not make excuses.

   _____

   _____

   _____

   _____

Focus on Community

Relationship Skills

Name: _____ Date: _____

Evaluating Consequences

Big decisions can be challenging. Communities need to think through big decisions. They need to analyze all the information carefully. They need to listen to experts and discuss all the options. All that information will help them make the best decisions.

Directions: Read each community decision. Write how it will affect people who live there, both positively and negatively.

1. The city council voted to install a stoplight at a busy intersection.

    Positive effects: _____

    _____

    Negative effects: _____

    _____

2. The county commission installed a skate park in a quiet neighborhood.

    Positive effects: _____

    _____

    Negative effects: _____

    _____

3. The town council passed an ordinance to allow backyard chickens.

    Positive effects: _____

    _____

    Negative effects: _____

    _____

Focus on Community — Responsible Decision-Making

Name: _____ **Date:** _____

Different Communities

Every state has a variety of communities, from small towns to large cities. Each corner of your state has something unique to offer. Every place has something that makes it special. They may all be different, but they also have a lot in common.

Directions: Compare and contrast your part of the state with another area that is totally different. Consider things such as population, open spaces, types of buildings, restaurants, shops, farms, traffic, and noise. Label the diagram below with both communities' names. Then, complete the Venn diagram. Conduct research as needed.

My Community: _____   Another Community: _____

Focus on State

Self-Awareness

Name:_____ Date:_____

Focus on State

Self-Management

Planning to Meet Goals

Everyone has problems. There are even problems that require cities or states to work together. When your state is working to solve a problem that seems enormous, you can still be part of the solution.

Directions: Read the scenario. Create a three-step plan to keep your school open. Then, answer the questions.

School in Trouble

Your state passed a new education requirement that all schools with test scores below a certain level will close at the end of the year. That's just one month away. You feel prepared for the test, but you also know that your school is on the list of those that may close. You also do not agree with the decision to close schools because of test scores.

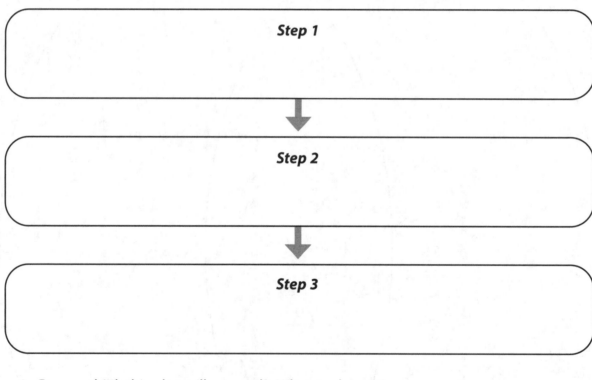

Step 1

Step 2

Step 3

1. Do you think this plan will succeed? Why or why not?

_____

_____

2. Who will need to help you for your plan to work?

_____

_____

Name:_____ Date:_____

Influences of Your Surroundings

Different families have different rules. Sometimes, those differences are based on where they live. Different states have different rules, too. Your surroundings can have a huge impact on the type of behavior that is and is not allowed.

Directions: Read the scenarios. Each person lives in a different part of the state. Explain how their surroundings might influence the rules.

1. Yvonne lives in the biggest city in the state. She is allowed to ride the city bus downtown with her older sister. She can walk alone to the corner store to buy snacks. She also walks to school with one of her friends. But she is not allowed to stay home alone for more than a few minutes. She attends an after-school program at the community center instead.

    _____

    _____

    _____

2. Ruthie lives in the suburbs. The only place she's allowed to go by herself is to the park across the street. A relative needs to drive her if she wants to go anywhere else. She goes to school on the bus. No one is home when she gets back from school, so she and her younger brother go inside and do their homework.

    _____

    _____

    _____

3. Ishaan lives in the country. He rides the bus to school because it's 10 miles from his house. But he can ride his bike to most of his friends' houses. As long as he's home for dinner, he can go out by himself after school or on the weekends.

    _____

    _____

    _____

    _____

Name: _____ Date: _____

Focus on State

Relationship Skills

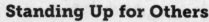

Standing Up for Others

If you pay attention, you will quickly see people in your state who are struggling. There are many ways to support those people. Gathering information is one way to begin. You can also speak up to inform people in charge about what is happening. You can even look for other concerned people and take action together.

Directions: Read the story, and answer the questions.

Helping Migrant Farm Workers

Sam lives in the southwestern United States. He has just learned about migrant workers at school. There are many migrant workers in his state who move from farm to farm for work. They are often paid less than minimum wage. They also have no job stability, which makes it hard to have a stable home. Sam would like to take action to stand up for migrant workers in his state.

1. What can Sam do on his own? List two specific actions he could take.

_____

_____

2. How can Sam connect with other people who want to help?

_____

_____

3. Draw how Sam can help.

Name: _____ Date: _____

Weighing Options

When making a big decision, it's important to think about all the possible outcomes. Listing the pros and cons can help. You can use it to consider all the positive and negative outcomes.

Directions: Your cousin's family is considering a move to your state. They've asked for your opinion. List at least five pros and five cons. Then, explain your final choice.

Pros	Cons

Focus on State

Responsible Decision-Making

1. Do you think they should move to your state? Why or why not?

_____

_____

_____

Name: _____ Date: _____

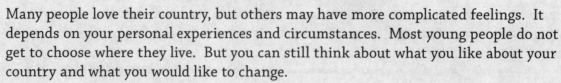

Focus on Country

Self-Awareness

Identifying Emotions

Many people love their country, but others may have more complicated feelings. It depends on your personal experiences and circumstances. Most young people do not get to choose where they live. But you can still think about what you like about your country and what you would like to change.

Directions: Describe four different emotions you feel when you think about your country. Explain why you feel each way.

I feel _____ because _____

_____

_____

I feel _____ because _____

_____

_____

I feel _____ because _____

_____

_____

I feel _____ because _____

_____

_____

Name: _____ Date: _____

Persistence

No one wins all the time. Everyone will lose eventually, and most people lose several times before they finally succeed. The key to long-term success is persistence. *Persistence* means you keep going and you don't give up.

Did you know that most U.S. presidents lost one or more big elections before becoming president? Lyndon B. Johnson lost a bid for the Senate. Richard Nixon lost a presidential race. Jimmy Carter and Bill Clinton each lost a governor's race. But they learned from each failure and did better the next time. That's persistence.

Directions: Answer the questions about a time you were persistent.

1. What were you trying to do?

_____

_____

2. What went wrong and why?

_____

_____

_____

3. How did you feel at the time?

_____

_____

4. Why didn't you give up?

_____

_____

5. How did you motivate yourself to keep going?

_____

_____

6. What was the end result?

_____

_____

_____

Focus on Country

Self-Management

Name: _____ Date: _____

Influences of the Government

You may not stop to think about how the U.S. government affects your everyday life. But it does! The rights and limits in the Constitution affect everyone in the United States. So do the laws passed by Congress.

Focus on Country
Social Awareness

Directions: List at least one way each of the following rights or laws affects your daily life.

1. You have the right to worship freely (or not worship at all).

_____
_____
_____

2. You can make choices about your healthcare and education.

_____
_____
_____

3. Medicines need to be tested to make sure they're safe and effective.

_____
_____
_____

4. Factories are not allowed to send certain pollutants into the air.

_____
_____
_____

5. People can speak out against leaders and laws they think are unfair.

_____
_____
_____

6. You have the right to attend school.

_____
_____
_____

Name: _____ Date: _____

Compromise

Many members of Congress disagree on several issues, but they still have to work together to pass laws. They use strategies such as compromise in order to get things done. A compromise is when each side gives up part of what they want in order to find a solution. It's like meeting in the middle.

Directions: Explain whether each scenario is a fair compromise. Then, answer the question.

1. The New Jersey Plan proposed that states get an equal number of representatives in Congress. The Virginia Plan proposed that the number of representatives be based on a state's population. The solution was to have two houses in Congress. The Senate has an equal number of senators from each state. The House of Representatives is based on population.

   _____

   _____

   _____

2. One group of senators wants to cut taxes by 20 percent. Another group wants to cut taxes by 10 percent. The first group outnumbers the second group, so the solution is an 18 percent tax cut.

   _____

   _____

   _____

3. Is compromising always a good idea? Why or why not?

   _____

   _____

   _____

   _____

Focus on Country
Relationship Skills

© Shell Education   126962—180 Days of Social-Emotional Learning   95

Name: _____ Date: _____

Analyzing Decisions

The bigger the decision, the more important it is to think about all the potential outcomes. Governments use teams of people to do this. Then, politicians and other officials debate those outcomes. This helps to ensure the best decision has been made. They also look back at past decisions to make predictions for the future.

Directions: Read the scenario. Answer the questions to evaluate the decision made by the U.S. government.

National Parks

Congress created the world's first national park in 1872. They turned 3,000 square miles (7,770 square kilometers) into Yellowstone National Park. Since then, they have created over 400 national park areas. The parks cover more than 83 million acres (336,000 square km). The parks help protect wildlife. They give people a chance to be outside. Other countries also now have national parks of their own.

1. How did the decision to create Yellowstone affect the people who lived near it?

   _____

   _____

2. How did the decision affect people in other parts of the country?

   _____

   _____

3. How did the decision affect local animals and plants?

   _____

   _____

4. How did the decision affect businesses near the park?

   _____

   _____

5. Do you think this was a good decision? Why or why not?

   _____

   _____

   _____

   _____

Name: _____ Date: _____

Integrating Identities

Everyone has overlapping identities. Part of your identity is based on your community (your city, town, or county). Part is based on your state. Part is based on your country. If you have ever moved, you also carry a part of your identity from one place to another.

Directions: Write or draw how each place has shaped your identity. Then, answer the questions.

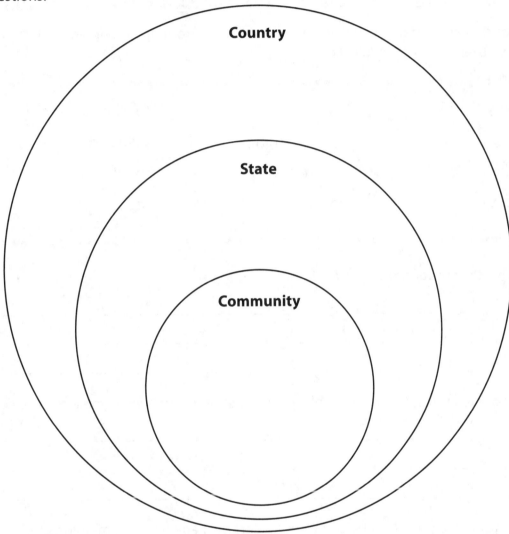

1. Circle three words that best represent you. Which circles are they in?

   _____

   _____

2. What does that tell you about your identity?

   _____

   _____

Focus on World
Self-Awareness

Name: _____ Date: _____

Trying New Things

Sometimes, people who are already famous for one thing try something completely different. Ronald Reagan was a famous actor before he became president. This kind of change does not always work out. Usain Bolt was a world-class sprinter. But he was not the best professional soccer player. Michael Jordan was one of the best basketball players. But he did not make it in professional baseball. No matter the outcome, it takes courage to try something new.

Directions: Circle something new you would like to try from the list, or write your own activities. Then, answer the questions.

archery	fencing	martial arts
baking	figure skating	painting
bowling	gymnastics	tennis
dancing	knitting	_____

1. Why do you want to try this?

   _____

   _____

   _____

2. What are at least two benefits of trying something new, even if you are not successful?

   _____

   _____

   _____

3. Why might a successful person want to start over again with something else?

   _____

   _____

   _____

Name: _____ **Date:** _____

Appreciating Differences

You might feel pressure to be like everybody else. Sometimes, people who do not fit in get teased. But there is so much diversity in the world that no two people can be exactly the same. It is great to celebrate the things that make you unique and different.

Directions: Denise wrote about originality in her journal. Read her text, and answer the questions.

Originality

In this world, there are few who can appreciate originality. And yet, there are few who do not crave it. Those who try to stand out, then mock those who also stand out, confuse me the most. If everyone in this world could appreciate each other's differences, we could make the world a better place.

Focus on World

Social Awareness

1. What do you think her text is saying?

_____

_____

_____

2. Do you agree with the message of the text? Why or why not?

_____

_____

_____

3. Who are some truly original people in the world? What makes them so unique?

_____

_____

_____

4. Are those people appreciated for their uniqueness? Why or why not?

_____

_____

_____

Name: _____ Date: _____

Exchange Programs

One way to build relationships with people from other countries is through exchange programs. Students from one country live with a family in another country. Sometimes, they stay a few weeks. Sometimes, they stay for a year or more.

Focus on World

Relationship Skills

Directions: Imagine you are hosting a foreign exchange student from another country. What American traditions, customs, or landmarks would you be most excited to show them? Write a paragraph describing what you would show them and why. Then, draw a picture to support your paragraph.

_____

_____

_____

_____

_____

_____

_____

_____

_____

_____

_____

Name: _____ Date: _____

Anticipating Consequences

It can be helpful to consider the consequences of your actions. For example, if you wake up late, you might get to school late. But consequences can be positive, too. If you are kind to a new student, you might make a new friend.

Directions: Write the possible consequences of each global choice.

Choice   **Consequences**

| Send food and medicine to developing nations |  | |

| Restrict immigration | → | |

| Eliminate trade between countries | → | |

| Allow people to move among countries freely | → | |

| Work with other countries to reduce car emissions | → | |

Focus on World

Responsible Decision-Making

Name: _____ Date: _____

Focus on Self

Self-Awareness

Examining Prejudices and Biases

It's nice to think that we don't have any prejudices or biases. But everyone does. Sometimes, these prejudiced thoughts are so automatic that you don't even notice them. One way to overcome biases is to try to notice when they pop into your head and push back against them. Students often sort each other into groups. Then, they make judgements based on things such as how others dress or who their friends are.

Directions: Think about the people in your school or community, and answer the questions.

1. What do you think of when you hear each of these terms?

   nerd _____

   cool kid _____

   athlete _____

   band kid _____

2. How else do people your age identify? Consider things such as appearance, grades, activities, clothes, or economic status.

   _____

   _____

   _____

   _____

3. Do you think it's fair to group people using any of the categories above? Why or why not?

   _____

   _____

   _____

   _____

4. What could you say to yourself when you notice yourself thinking about other kids in a biased way?

   _____

   _____

   _____

   _____

Name: _____ Date: _____

Self-Motivation

It can be hard to keep going when you have a lot of responsibilities. It's good to have a menu of strategies you can use to motivate yourself. One strategy is to keep motivational reminders handy. They may be visual reminders, such as posters.

Directions: Create a motivational poster for yourself for the week ahead. Think of all the activities and schoolwork you have to do. Use pictures and words. Be as creative as you like.

Focus on Self

Self-Management

Name: _____ Date: _____

Focus on Self

Social Awareness

Complimenting Others

Giving compliments is a great way to build relationships. You can tell someone what you appreciate about them. You can thank someone for being helpful. Authentic compliments are specific and personal.

Directions: Write a compliment for each scenario. Be sure to make your compliments specific and personal.

1. A new student at your school was just elected class president. Her speech before the election was so powerful that some people cried.

   _____

   _____

   _____

2. One of your family members performed in a talent show. He got a standing ovation. You didn't even realize that he played the piano!

   _____

   _____

   _____

3. Someone your age just moved in next door. You've seen them practicing skateboarding in the driveway. They're really good!

   _____

   _____

   _____

4. Your aunt had a painting displayed in the community art show. Her painting was really colorful and bright. It was your favorite piece in the entire show.

   _____

   _____

   _____

5. Your neighbor made some cookies. They are all different shapes and iced individually. She even wrote little messages with icing on each cookie. You think they look nice enough to come from a bakery.

   _____

   _____

   _____

 126962—180 Days of Social-Emotional Learning

Name: _____ **Date:** _____

I-Messages

It's easy for conversations to get off track when strong emotions are involved. If you want to express how you are feeling, it's better to use an I-message. I-messages avoid blaming others for your feelings. You can say, "I feel frustrated right now." A blaming statement would say "You're so frustrating." I-messages are much easier for people to hear and process. When people feel blamed, they get defensive.

Directions: Read each scenario. Rewrite the blaming statement as an I-message.

1. You are working on a project with Xavier. He is distracted and not helping much. You are getting angry because there is so much work left to do.

    "Stop being so lazy! You're driving me crazy!"

    _____

    _____

2. You're eating dinner with your family. One of your family members is talking loudly. You have a bad headache.

    "Would you please stop talking? You're giving me a headache!"

    _____

    _____

3. Your friend borrowed your bike yesterday. When she brought it back, it had a dent and a flat tire.

    "You ruined my bike! You're so irresponsible!"

    _____

    _____

4. You're excited to try your aunt's cookies. But when you go to get one, you see that your cousin has just eaten the last one.

    "You ate the last one? I didn't even get to try any. You're so rude!"

    _____

    _____

Name: _____ Date: _____

Focus on Self

Responsible Decision-Making

Fight, Flight, or Freeze

Conflict is a fact of life, but dealing with conflict can be tricky. Many people would prefer to avoid it altogether. In general, people tend to have an automatic fight, flight, or freeze response to conflict. They may gear up for a fight or argument. They may try to escape the conflict by physically leaving or by giving up. Or they may freeze and refuse to get involved or not know what to say. None of these approaches is especially useful. It is better to stay calm and talk to each other.

Directions: Answer the questions about how you approach conflict in your life.

1. What words come to mind when you think about conflict? Write at least three.

   _____

   _____

2. How does it make you feel to be involved in a conflict? Think about physical changes or any specific emotions that arise.

   _____

   _____

   _____

3. What is your natural response when someone is angry with you? Do you leave? Freeze? Stay calm and talk?

   _____

   _____

4. What is your natural response when you are angry with someone else? Describe your physical and emotional responses.

   _____

   _____

   _____

5. How might you calm down when you feel like you want to fight, flight, or freeze?

   _____

   _____

   _____

Name: _____ Date: _____

Core Values

Recall that core values are beliefs or ideals that are important to a person or group. Families have core values. You might not talk about them directly. But you can probably identify your family's core values. Think about how you have been taught to behave and what lessons your family has emphasized.

Directions: In medieval times, powerful families had their own family crests. These crests were placed on shields and flags. They often included symbols that represented the family. Create your own family crest. In each quadrant, include words and symbols showing your family's core values.

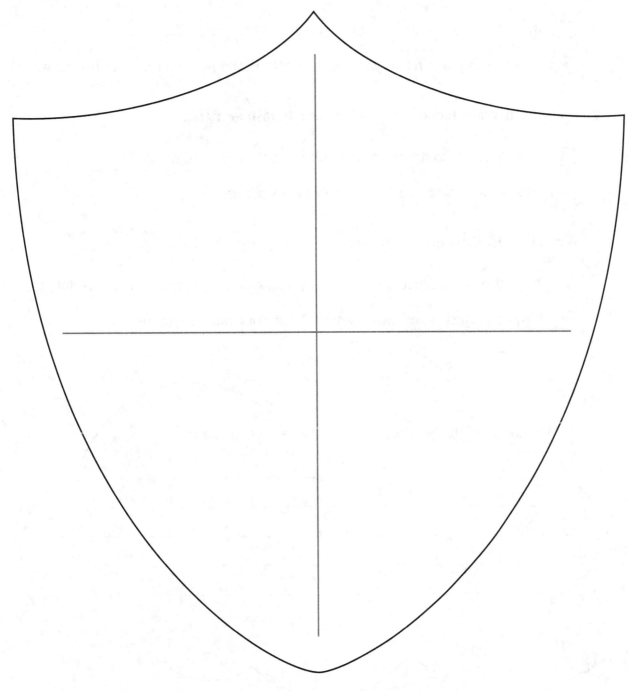

Name:_____ Date:_____

Focus on Family
Self-Management

Managing Your Emotions

Emotions can feel powerful, and they can also be overwhelming. You can observe them and see where they take you, or you can use your own thoughts to influence your emotions. This is a form of self-coaching or self-talk.

Directions: Fill in the bubble of the self-talk message that each person should use to feel better. Then, answer the question.

1. Erica's brother gets to move into the old guest room. She still has to share a bedroom with her sister.

   (A) It's not fair! He always gets the biggest and the best stuff.

   (B) It's annoying, but in two years he'll be off to college, and I can have his room.

2. Ryan's mom asked him to start taking out the trash every night.

   (A) Why do I have to do it? I have to do everything around here.

   (B) I don't want to do it, but it will only take a minute.

3. Manuel's older sister gets to stay up an hour later than he does.

   (A) At least I don't have to get up as early as she does to catch the high school bus.

   (B) Why can't I just set my own bedtime? I'm not a baby anymore.

What do all of the helpful messages above have in common?

_____
_____
_____
_____

Name: _____ Date: _____

Planning

Families need to do a lot of planning. You might have family events that you have to attend. Or you might need transportation to or from an activity or event. It's important to communicate in advance so you won't be disappointed.

Directions: Read the texts, and answer the question.

Trip to the Movies

You are trying to plan a time to go see a movie with friends on Saturday. The theater is about 15 minutes from your home. You need an adult to drive you there and bring you home. Movie times are 11:00 a.m., 1:00 p.m., 3:00 p.m., 5:00 p.m., and 7:00 p.m. The movie is two hours long.

Family Events

Your cousin has a soccer game at 10:00 a.m. You are expected to attend. You have a doctor appointment at 12:00 p.m. in a town 30 minutes away. Your parent is having friends over for dinner at 8:00 p.m. They need about two hours to prepare for the dinner, and they want you to help.

1. Which movie time should you choose? Why?

_____

_____

_____

Focus on Family
Social Awareness

Name:_____ Date:_____

Focus on Family

Relationship Skills

Communicating Effectively

There are many ways to help communication or to block it. You can use your words. But you can also help or block communication by the way you speak and by the nonverbal cues you give. It's easy to ruin a conversation accidentally with these blockers. If you're not paying attention, you might not even realize that you're doing it.

Directions: Decide whether each action is a helper or a blocker, and write it in the correct column. Then, answer the questions.

Actions

nodding to show agreement	looking at your phone while someone is talking
avoiding eye contact with the person speaking	making eye contact
smiling	speaking clearly
interrupting	mumbling
not responding	rolling your eyes

Helpers	Blockers

1. How do you feel when someone uses communication helpers with you?

_____

_____

2. How do you feel when someone uses communication blockers with you?

_____

_____

Name: _____ **Date:** _____

Identifying Solutions

Some problems are easy to solve. If you're hungry, you can have a snack. Other problems are more complicated. Sometimes, you need to gather more information or ask someone for help before making a decision. When in doubt, it's always good to ask for help.

Directions: Read the story, and answer the questions.

Home Alone

It's 10:30 a.m. on Saturday morning. Taylor is at home alone while her parent goes to the grocery store. Suddenly, the doorbell rings. Taylor knows that she is not supposed to answer the door when she's home alone. But the man at the door is wearing a uniform and appears to be from the gas company. She is worried that it could be something urgent. He rings the bell again. She's not sure what to do.

1. What is the problem in this story?

_____

_____

2. What information does Taylor need to solve this problem?

_____

_____

3. How could Taylor get that information?

_____

_____

_____

4. What should Taylor do? Why?

_____

_____

_____

_____

Name:_____ Date:_____

Focus on Community

Self-Awareness

Time Capsules

Have you ever wondered what people in the future will think of the world we live in today? Sometimes, people create time capsules. These are collections of objects that show what life was like in a particular time and place.

Directions: Imagine your community is putting together a time capsule. The goal is to capture what life is like for students in your community right now. Draw or write the objects you would include. Then, answer the question.

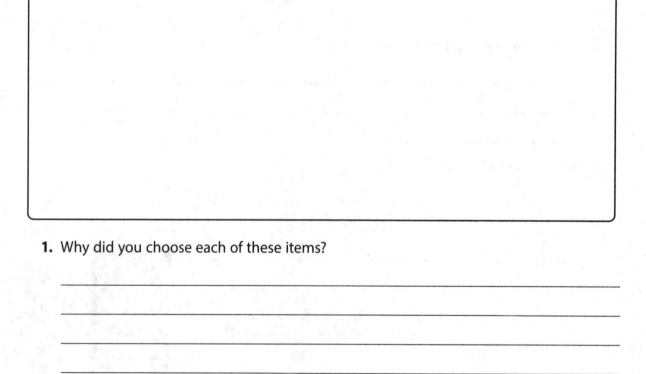

1. Why did you choose each of these items?

_____

_____

_____

_____

_____

126962—180 Days of Social-Emotional Learning   © Shell Education

Name: _____ Date: _____

Checklists

Checklists can be very useful tools. They can help you identify tasks that need to be done. They can help you keep track of which tasks have been completed. Hospitals use checklists to make sure everything is done safely and properly and that everyone receives proper care. Teachers use checklists to help students track their work. You can use checklists to manage your own tasks.

Directions: Write the name of a place in your community that is used by many people, such as a park. What kinds of things should people do before they arrive there? What might they need to bring or prepare in advance? What kinds of things should people do before they leave that place? How can they keep it clean? Write two checklists people could use.

Focus on Community

Self-Management

Before You Arrive

☐ _____

_____

☐ _____

_____

☐ _____

_____

☐ _____

_____

☐ _____

_____

☐ _____

_____

☐ _____

_____

Before You Leave

☐ _____

_____

☐ _____

_____

☐ _____

_____

☐ _____

_____

☐ _____

_____

☐ _____

_____

☐ _____

_____

Name: _____ Date: _____

Taking Others' Perspectives

Many places and resources in your community are used by more than one group. Families come to the park to play, but so do adults who like to jog. It's important to be sensitive to the perspectives of different groups. People can share the resources as long as they are respectful to each other.

Directions: Read the story. Then, write what each group could say to one of the other groups to express what they are feeling.

Rumble at the Park

There are three groups of people who regularly use the town park. Families with young children come to use the fenced playground. But the fence doesn't always get closed, and toys roll out. Adults and teenagers come to play pickup basketball in the evenings. They often play loud music. Sometimes, that music contains words that are inappropriate for young children. Dog owners bring their dogs to play and sometimes let them off leash. Occasionally, the dogs run onto the basketball court or the playground. People get very upset when this happens.

Families talking to dog owners:

I feel _____ because _____

_____

Basketball players talking to families:

I feel _____ because _____

_____

Dog owners talking to basketball players:

I feel _____ because _____

_____

Families talking to basketball players:

I feel _____ because _____

_____

Communicating Effectively

When there is a disagreement or a conflict, it can be hard to communicate. It's easy to start accusing and blaming the other side. But that is not helpful.

Directions: Read each scenario. Rewrite each quotation so that it does not blame or accuse someone else.

1. Jim lives next door to Bill. After a recent snowstorm, Bill blew snow onto Jim's driveway. Jim yelled at him, "Quit blowing snow onto my driveway! You're causing me extra work for no reason!"

   _____

   _____

   _____

2. Coral was walking her puppy when it escaped from the leash and ran through Mrs. Wilson's flower beds. Mrs. Wilson was furious and said, "You don't care about your neighbors at all! Get that rude dog out of here!"

   _____

   _____

   _____

3. Mr. Frank often parks his car so that it blocks a portion of Mrs. Kim's driveway. Usually it's not a big deal, but today Mrs. Kim was running late and exploded. She marched over to Mr. Frank's house and said, "You are so selfish! You always block our driveway and never think about anyone but yourself!"

   _____

   _____

   _____

Focus on Community

Relationship Skills

Name: _____ Date: _____

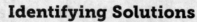

Focus on Communtiy

Responsible Decision-Making

Identifying Solutions

Win-win solutions are obviously the best for everyone. But they can be hard to find. It can sometimes seem like no solution will make everyone happy. It takes creativity to find a compromise that will make everyone in a community happy.

Directions: Read each scenario, and answer the questions.

Hunters want to be allowed to hunt in the conservation land. But other people like to hike and bike in that area and are afraid that hunting would make it unsafe for them to enjoy it.

1. Who are the two parties involved, and what does each want?

   _____

   _____

   _____

2. Is there a way to compromise?

   _____

   _____

   _____

Two different community groups want to use the meeting room at the library at the same time every week.

3. Who are the two parties involved, and what does each want?

   _____

   _____

   _____

4. Is there a way to compromise?

   _____

   _____

   _____

Name: _____ Date: _____

Examining Stereotypes

Stereotypes are assumptions that people make about a group of people. In some countries, there is a stereotype that all Americans are rich. Obviously, that is not true. There are stereotypes about people based on their race, religion, gender, and many other things. Sometimes, a stereotype can even sound like a positive generalization. But all stereotypes can be harmful.

Directions: Answer the questions.

1. Write your own definition of what a stereotype is.

   _____

   _____

   _____

2. How are stereotypes hurtful?

   _____

   _____

   _____

   _____

3. How might stereotypes affect the way you think about different people?

   _____

   _____

   _____

   _____

4. Write at least two positive things you can say or think the next time you hear a stereotype.

   _____

   _____

   _____

   _____

Focus on State
Self-Awareness

Name: _____ Date: _____

Focus on State

Self-Management

Managing Emotions

Competitions can be fun and exciting. But they can also make you feel nervous and stressed. You can use stress-reduction techniques when you're feeling nervous. You will feel better, and you will perform better.

Directions: Write at least one way Crystal could use each strategy to calm herself down.

Track the Nerves

Crystal is on the track team. She has practiced three days a week all year and won every meet she entered. Her team made it to the state championships. But she's nervous. She bombed her first event. She got a cramp partway through and couldn't finish strong. That never happens to her! Today, she has two more events: her favorite individual event and the team relay. The team is really counting on her, which just makes her feel more nervous.

Self-Talk

Mindfulness Techniques

Things That Make Her Happy

Name: _____ Date: _____

Taking Others' Perspectives

Sometimes, a group or side will "win" a conflict, or get what it wants. Sometimes, it won't. Remember to consider how the other side feels, especially when you're on the winning side.

Directions: Read the scenario, and answer the questions.

Focus on State

Social Awareness

Planes or Trains?

Your state is expanding its public transportation system. State leaders are considering two plans. One plan would create a high-speed train route to connect two major cities in your state. The other plan would build an airport in the part of the state where you live. You are really hoping they build an airport so that you can visit out-of-state family more often. But people who live in the two large cities are hoping they choose the high-speed train. After much debate, state leaders decide to build the airport.

1. How would you feel about this decision? Why?

   _____

   _____

   _____

2. How would people in the two major cities feel? Explain.

   _____

   _____

   _____

3. How would you feel if the train had been built instead?

   _____

   _____

   _____

4. If the leaders had chosen to build the train route, how would you hope the people in the two major cities would react?

   _____

   _____

   _____

Name: _____ Date: _____

Focus on State
Relationship Skills

Communicating with Social Media

Social media is a popular way to communicate. Adults and kids both use it, though maybe in different ways. Your state leaders use social media, too. It's a way to share positive news and important information. It's another way for state leaders to stay connected to the people who live there.

Directions: Imagine that you are the social media manager for your state. Create four engaging posts that would help residents feel good about living there. Your audience is primarily the residents of your state.

Name: _____ Date: _____

Anticipating and Evaluating Consequences

It is important to think about all the possible outcomes of a decision. It is even more important when that decision could affect thousands or even millions of people. This is why it takes a lot of time for state leaders to make decisions.

Directions: Read each potential decision. Answer the questions.

A community group is urging the state to raise the minimum wage by 50 percent.

1. What are the positive consequences, and who would be affected?

_____

_____

_____

2. What are the negative consequences, and who would be affected?

_____

_____

_____

A community group is asking lawmakers to pass a law that sets a 6 p.m. curfew on all kids under 13.

3. What are the positive consequences, and who would be affected?

_____

_____

_____

4. What are the negative consequences, and who would be affected?

_____

_____

_____

Focus on State

Responsible Decision-Making

Name: _____ Date: _____

Focus on Country

Self-Awareness

Core Values

Decisions often reflect our values and priorities. Our most important beliefs should guide our choices. That's often true for countries, as well. You can often look at decisions made by your country and identify the values they were trying to uphold.

Directions: Review common decisions made by the United States. Consider which values were driving each decision. Complete the graphic organizer by using some of the values in the box, or adding your own.

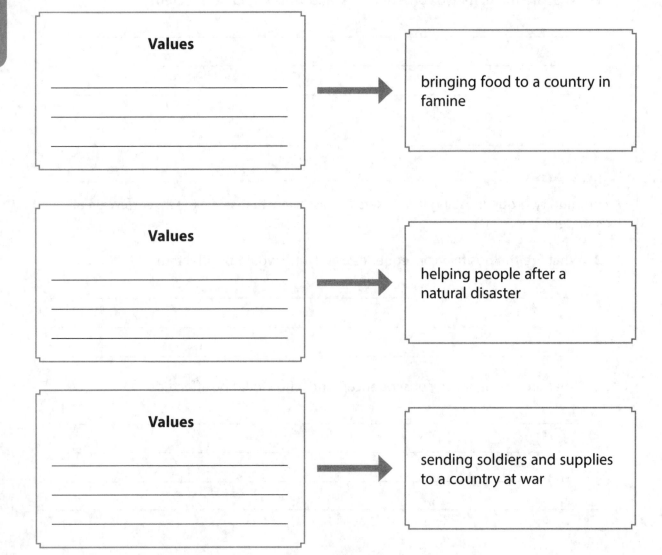

American Values

compassion   freedom

democracy   independence

equality   justice

Values

_____

_____

_____

→ bringing food to a country in famine

Values

_____

_____

_____

→ helping people after a natural disaster

Values

_____

_____

_____

→ sending soldiers and supplies to a country at war

Name: _____ Date: _____

Getting Involved

It might feel good to complain. But it feels even better to think about what you can do to help make things better. Adult citizens can help make things better by voting in elections. But you can help, too! You can raise awareness and educate people about issues that are important to you. You can write to your representatives. You can also volunteer and get involved in service projects.

Focus on Country

Self-Management

Directions: On the left side, list five problems in this country. On the right side, write two steps you could take to help address each issue.

Problems   **What I Can Do**

Name: _____ Date: _____

Focus on Country
Social Awareness

Taking Others' Perspectives

The United States is a country built on immigration. Everyone except American Indians came to the United States from somewhere else. But it was not easy, and it was not always by choice. Even today, immigrants continue to come. They enrich our country with new perspectives and new skills.

Directions:. Complete the web to consider what it's like to be an immigrant in the United States. Conduct research as needed.

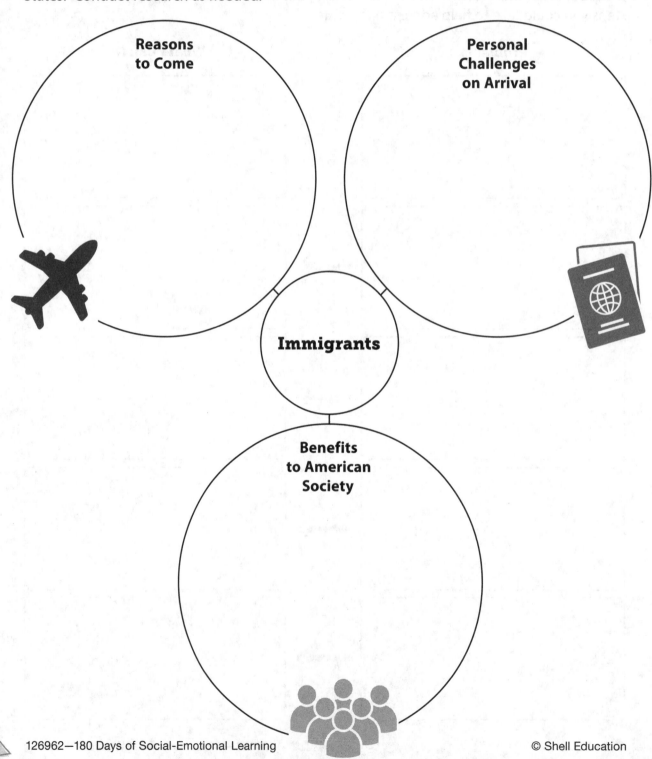

Name: _____ **Date:** _____

Types of Communication

It used to take weeks—sometimes months—to send a letter from one part of the United States to another. Communication has improved dramatically since then. Now, there are so many ways to send messages and information instantly. But every method has its pros and cons.

Directions: List a different communication method in each speech bubble. Then, write one benefit and one drawback of each type of communication.

Name:_____ Date:_____

Identifying Solutions

Every year, the president gives a speech to describe the state of the country and their goals for the next year. It's called the State of the Union Address. Sometimes, it is a positive, uplifting speech. Other times, it is full of warnings of the dangers the nation faces. The tone of the speech reflects what the president thinks of where the country is and where they want it to go.

Directions: Imagine you are the president. Answer these questions about your State of the Union Address. Then, draw yourself giving your speech.

1. What tone will the speech have? Are you uplifting, or do you have warnings? Why?

_____

_____

_____

2. What big points will you make about the current conditions in the United States?

_____

_____

_____

3. What goals do you have for the next year?

_____

_____

_____

Focus on Country

Responsible Decision-Making

© Shell Education

Name: _____ Date: _____

Describing World Cultures

Humans have been watching the stars since the beginning of time. We have dreamed about distant places in the universe. We've wondered if there is other intelligent life out there somewhere. If there were aliens we could communicate with, what would we want them to know about humans, our cultures, and our planet?

Directions: Imagine that we have made contact with aliens at last. Write and draw to show what images, videos, sounds, music, or words you would send them to help understand our world. Then, answer the question.

Focus on World

Self-Awareness

Images	Sounds/Music

Videos	Words

1. What might the aliens think about humans based on your choices?

_____

_____

_____

Name: _____ Date: _____

Taking Action

It can be easy to feel overwhelmed when you think about a problem that affects the whole world. But there is often something you can do to help. You can overcome the feeling of helplessness by doing something. Even the smallest actions can have a great impact.

Directions: Add as many additional problems and actions as you can to the lists. Then, answer the questions.

Problems	Actions
homelessness	write a letter to your senator
poverty	organize a food drive

1. Choose one world problem: _____

2. What action could you take to address it?

_____

_____

3. Why is this the best choice?

_____

_____

_____

Taking Others' Perspectives

Every country has problems, but they are not all the same. It's important to think about what people in other countries experience and how they might be feeling. It might be quite different from the life you live.

Directions: Read each scenario, and answer the questions.

1. A country's government has been overthrown by the military. How might the people who live in that country feel? Why?

_____

_____

_____

2. A country is thriving economically, but their neighboring country is not. How might the people in each country feel? Why?

_____

_____

_____

3. There are tanks in the streets and strict curfews in place. Schools are closed. How might the people who live in that country feel? Why?

_____

_____

_____

4. Thousands of refugees are pouring in from one country into another, looking for assistance. How might the people in each country feel? Why?

_____

_____

_____

Focus on World

Social Awareness

Name:_____ Date:_____

Focus on World

Relationship Skills

Cultural Competency

The arts can be powerful methods of communication. Music, visual arts, theater, movies, and literature are all good ways to tell a story. The arts can help build a bridge between people from different cultures. They can make people feel something. They can help increase understanding.

Directions: List at least three works of art that you like in each category. Describe how each one made you feel. Then, answer the question.

Songs

Movies/Plays

Literature/Visual Arts

1. Circle the work of art that moved you the most or that means the most to you. What made it special? What did you learn from it?

_____

_____

_____

_____

Identifying Solutions

Recall that big problems require outside help. Small problems are those that you can handle yourself. The same is true for international problems. Big problems require a large group of countries and high-level leaders to resolve. Small problems are less complicated. They can be resolved by lower-level representatives from each country.

Focus on World

Responsible Decision-Making

Directions: Circle whether each conflict is high-level or low-level, and explain why.

1. Several countries border the same sea. Pollution from many factories and farms in each country has contaminated the sea. Fish and other sea life have been dying. They have not been able to decide on a solution.

   high-level   low-level

   _____

   _____

   _____

2. Two countries are separated by a wide river. They both want to build a bridge across it, and they have agreed where to build it. But they need to coordinate who will build it and how it will be funded.

   high-level   low-level

   _____

   _____

   _____

3. One country created a new medicine. That country is the only one with the formula to make it. The materials for the medicine are only found in another country. Every country in the world needs the medicine as soon as possible.

   high-level   low-level

   _____

   _____

   _____

Name: _____ Date: _____

Focus on Self

Self-Awareness

Growth Mindset

The way you think about your brain matters. If you think of your abilities and intelligence as fixed and unchanging, then you will have a hard time when problems arise. You will be more likely to give up and less likely to learn. That is called a *fixed mindset*. But you can develop a *growth mindset* instead. That is the belief that your intelligence and abilities can grow and improve. The most important qualities are your persistence and your effort.

Directions: Circle whether each person has a fixed mindset or growth mindset. Then, write at least one thing they could do to improve their mindset.

1. Chris has never thought he was good at math. It's always been confusing to him. So, he stopped trying to figure out math problems on his own. He just waits for the teacher to show them the right answer and writes it in his notebook. He usually passes the tests, but just barely.

   fixed mindset   growth mindset

   _____

   _____

2. Diamond does not think she is an athlete. In first grade, she played soccer and scored two goals on her own team. It was humiliating! So, she quit. In second grade, she tried gymnastics. But she fell off the balance beam and broke her arm on the first day. So, she quit. She's just not meant to do sports.

   fixed mindset   growth mindset

   _____

   _____

3. Marcus struggles with writing. He has a hard time organizing his thoughts. Marcus asked his older brother for help. His brother showed him how to outline his paragraphs before writing. It really helped Marcus organize his ideas before he wrote.

   fixed mindset   growth mindset

   _____

   _____

Name: _____ Date: _____

Perseverance

When things don't go your way, it can be quite easy to become discouraged. Even though you may feel terrible, the way you respond is very important. If you focus on negative thoughts, you might give up. Instead, give yourself a pep talk and keep trying.

Directions: Complete the flowchart about a time when you worked hard, but things did not go as you planned or hoped.

What happened?

How did you feel?

Did you keep trying or give up? Why?

What did you say (or could have said) to yourself to keep a positive outlook?

Self-Management

Focus on Self

Name: _____ Date: _____

Focus on Self

Social Awareness

Sympathy

Sympathy is when you show support for another person's misfortune. It's a way to acknowledge that someone else is having a hard time. It is also a powerful way to show someone that you care.

Directions: Read each scenario, and answer the questions.

Annabelle's father made a special dessert for her birthday, but it turned out terribly. Her brother spit out his first bite. Nobody could eat it.

1. How does Annabelle's father feel?

_____

_____

_____

2. How could Annabelle express sympathy?

_____

_____

_____

_____

Kate's friend, Rachel, came to school crying. Her cat died the night before.

3. How does Rachel feel?

_____

_____

_____

4. How could Kate express sympathy?

_____

_____

_____

_____

Name: _____ Date: _____

Developing Positive Relationships

You probably have more people in your life who support you than you realize. Everywhere you go, you are building relationships with other people. Some of those are close relationships, such as your close friends or family members. Some of those are not so close, such as the students you only see on the school bus or in the hallway. But each of them can offer you something, even if it's just a laugh or a wave now and then.

Directions: Complete the boxes with names of people you know in each category. Add categories and people you know from those categories to the empty boxes. Then, answer the questions.

Close Friends	

Close Family	

Other Family	

1. Which of these relationships is most important to you? Why?

   _____

   _____

2. Which of these relationships do you wish was stronger? How could you make that happen?

   _____

   _____

Name: _____ Date: _____

Identifying Solutions

There are many ways to solve a problem or make it go away. But not all solutions are equal. Some solutions are *constructive*, which means that they help build relationships or improve the person's life. Others are *destructive*, which means they can tear down relationships or make the person's life worse.

Directions: Identify the character's solution to each problem. Circle whether it was constructive or destructive.

1. Niam has a sore leg. He chose to ignore it and went skateboarding with his friends. He had fun, but hurt his leg even more, and now he has to sit out during his championship lacrosse game.

   Solution: _____

   constructive   destructive

2. Juanita was falling behind in science class. She asked a friend to tutor her and help prepare for the next test. She missed a party she really wanted to attend so that she could study. But she got a B on her test.

   Solution: _____

   constructive   destructive

3. Duncan was excited to spend his birthday money on a video game that he had wanted for months. But his friends convinced him to buy a different game instead. It turned out to be really disappointing.

   Solution: _____

   constructive   destructive

4. Kwame stayed up late three nights in a row to finish a great book he was reading. Then, he fell asleep during homeroom and failed a math test even though he studied.

   Solution: _____

   constructive   destructive

Name: _____ **Date:** _____

Identifying Emotions

Anger is a strong emotion that can be hard to control. Anger can even feel scary. But you can usually identify when anger starts to build inside you if you pay attention to your body and your emotions. Then, you can decide how to address it in a constructive way before it gets out of control.

Directions: Think of two times when you felt angry with a friend or classmate. Answer the questions for each one.

What happened?

_____

_____

Why did you feel angry?

_____

_____

How did you express your anger?

_____

_____

What happened?

_____

_____

Why did you feel angry?

_____

_____

How did you express your anger?

_____

_____

Focus on Friends

Self-Awareness

Name: _____ Date: _____

Managing One's Emotions

Everyone worries or feels anxious sometimes. One way to address your worries is to think about the worst and best things that could happen. Then, think about how likely each thing is to happen. In most cases, the best case scenario is more likely to happen than the worst case scenario.

Focus on Friends

Self-Management

Directions: Imagine you've been invited to a friend's party. Most of the other guests are people you don't really know. You are nervous and consider not going at all. Answer the questions about this situation.

1. What is the best possible outcome if you go to the party?

   _____

   _____

   _____

2. What is the worst possible outcome if you go to the party?

   _____

   _____

   _____

3. Which one is more likely to happen? Why?

   _____

   _____

   _____

   _____

4. What solution do you think is best? Why?

   _____

   _____

   _____

   _____

   _____

Name:_____ Date:_____

Understanding Others' Perspectives

Problems between friends can be tricky. It is not always clear which side is right and which is wrong. There are simply too many sides to every problem. To get along, it's important to understand other people's perspectives.

Directions: Read the story. Write the perspectives of both sides in the speech bubbles. Then, answer the question.

Hockey Friends

Parker, Aaron, and Rafael have been best friends since second grade. They did everything together, except for sports. Parker and Aaron play hockey. Rafael doesn't play any sports. But they all love the same video games and live in the same neighborhood.

When they started sixth grade, everything was the same. But after a month or two, Rafael noticed that Parker and Aaron seemed to be busy a lot on the weekends. Then, other hockey players started sitting with them at lunch. One day, when Rafael got to the lunch table, there was no room left for him. Parker shrugged and told him there was no room. Aaron looked away. As Rafael walked away, he heard laughter.

Parker & Aaron   **Rafael**

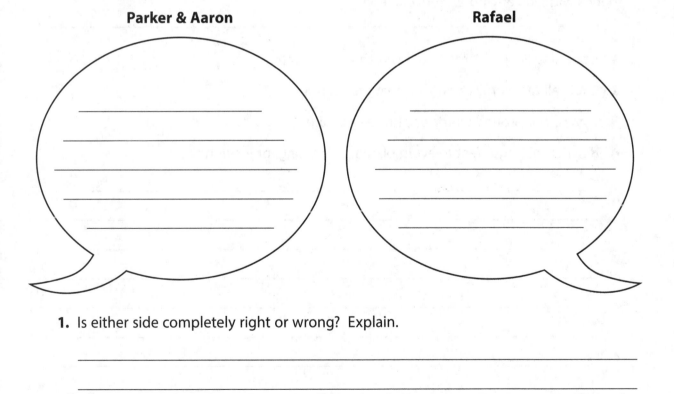

1. Is either side completely right or wrong? Explain.

_____

_____

_____

_____

Name: _____ Date: _____

Focus on Friends

Relationship Skills

Communicating Effectively

When you're arguing with a friend, it can be easy to say something you will regret. People often make statements that blame or accuse the other person of doing something. Then, they might insult each other. This can cause a conflict to *escalate*, which means to get worse. To avoid this, you should not blame, accuse, or insult another person during an argument.

Directions: Read the story, and then follow the steps.

The Secret

Lisa and Whitney are fighting. Lisa thinks that Whitney shared an embarrassing secret with several of their friends.

"I can't believe you told them about the time I got caught cheating on my math test!" Lisa says. "That was a secret! Now, they all think I'm an idiot, and it's all your fault. You're the worst friend ever."

Whitney tries to explain that she hadn't told them anything. But Lisa won't listen.

"I can't believe you're blaming this on me," Whitney says. "You always think the worst of me. You never believe anything I say. No wonder they don't want to be friends with you anymore. You're a jerk!"

1. Underline all the words or phrases that are blaming.

2. Circle all the words or phrases that are accusing.

3. Draw a box around words or phrases that are insults.

4. Rewrite this argument to avoid blaming, accusing, or insulting.

_____

_____

_____

_____

_____

_____

_____

_____

_____

_____

Name: _____ Date: _____

Weighing Risk and Reward

Making decisions often requires you to evaluate the risks and rewards of each choice. If the reward is worth the risk, then it might be a good choice. If the risk is not worth the reward, then you should think twice before doing it.

Directions: Read each scenario. Answer the questions.

Your friends want you to sneak into an R-rated movie after buying tickets to a G-rated film.

1. What is the risk?

   _____

2. What is the reward?

   _____

3. Is it worth it? Why or why not?

   _____

Your friends want you to go sledding on a private golf course because the best hill in town is there.

4. What is the risk?

   _____

5. What is the reward?

   _____

6. Is it worth it? Why or why not?

   _____

7. Write about a time you had to weigh risk and reward. What did you decide to do? Was it worth the risk?

   _____

   _____

   _____

   _____

   _____

Responsible Decision-Making

Focus on Friends

Name: _____ Date: _____

Self-Efficacy

Every community has resources available to help the people who live there. But people don't always know where to find them. Knowing where to go when you need help is an important skill.

Directions: Write the name or job title of someone in your community who could help with each situation.

1. How do I get help if I'm feeling depressed or anxious?

   _____

2. How do I get help if I need food assistance?

   _____

3. How do I find a way to get active or exercise?

   _____

4. How do I get a new pet?

   _____

5. How do I get help in an emergency?

   _____

6. How do I get help with schoolwork?

   _____

7. How do I find ways to volunteer?

   _____

Focus on Community

Self-Awareness

Name: _____ Date: _____

Planning and Organizing

Large events require a lot of planning. It is important to think through every aspect of an event. First, identify the necessary tasks. Then, assign each task to someone. Finally, stay organized and keep track as tasks are completed.

Directions: Imagine you are planning a neighborhood party. You have a committee of people to help you. Use words and pictures to list all the necessary tasks in each category.

Food and Drinks

Entertainment

Setup

Cleanup

Focus on Community

Self-Management

Name: _____ Date: _____

Focus on Community

Social Awareness

Expressing Gratitude

Gratitude is good for everyone. When people are thanked, they appreciate it. You can also make yourself feel good by stopping to think about what you're grateful for. It can improve your mood and your outlook on life. Developing a daily gratitude practice is a lifelong skill.

Directions: List five things you are grateful for in your community. Explain why you are grateful for each. Then, draw a picture of one of the things you listed.

1. I am grateful for _____

because _____

2. I am grateful for _____

because _____

3. I am grateful for _____

because _____

4. I am grateful for _____

because _____

5. I am grateful for _____

because _____

Name: _____ Date: _____

Communicating Effectively

People may sometimes deal with conflict by being passive-aggressive. It's one of several less effective ways to deal with conflict. Passive-aggressive communication is not direct. You don't tell someone you disagree with them. You might do something else to annoy them instead. Maybe you leave a chore undone. Or you "forget" to return a friend's message. A healthier way to deal with conflict is to be assertive. Directly express how you are feeling in a respectful manner.

Directions: Read each scenario, and circle whether the response is passive-aggressive or assertive. Then, answer the question.

1. Simon's neighbor keeps letting his dog poop in Simon's yard. Simon decides to blow his leaves into his neighbor's yard in return.

    passive-aggressive   assertive

2. Tuan's neighbor always leaves his trash cans out on the sidewalk for at least three days after trash day. Sometimes, they roll onto Tuan's driveway and block her entrance. Tuan sends the neighbor a polite message to explain why it's a problem.

    passive-aggressive   assertive

3. Marcy has had many issues with her mail carrier. She never remembers to close the mailbox. And she often fails to pick up the outgoing mail. Marcy leaves instructions on how to close her mailbox taped to the outside of it.

    passive-aggressive   assertive

4. Paolo and Miguel like to play basketball in their driveway. The seven-year-old who lives down the street often comes to play with them. He's nice, but he messes up their game. Paolo and Miguel start faking reasons to go inside every time the boy arrives.

    passive-aggressive   assertive

5. Choose one passive-aggressive example. Write an assertive response instead.

    _____

    _____

    _____

Name: _____ Date: _____

Focus on Community

Responsible Decision-Making

Role Models

A role model is someone who others look up to as an example of how they should be. A role model can be someone famous, such as an actor or a politician. Or they can be a person who is close to you, such as a family member or a teacher. You can be a role model, too. In fact, you may already be a role model to someone else.

Directions: Answer the questions.

1. Who are your role models? Why do you look up to them?

_____

_____

_____

2. Who sees you as their role model? Why do you they look up to you?

_____

_____

_____

3. What makes someone a good role model?

_____

_____

_____

4. Do you have to be perfect to be a good role model? Why or why not?

_____

_____

_____

© Shell Education

Name: _____ Date: _____

Understanding Where You Live

People may not know as much as they think about their home states. Now is your chance to learn some lesser-known facts about your state and teach your friends and family a thing or two at the same time.

Directions: Research and find four facts that are not commonly known about your state. Write a trivia quiz based on those facts. List the questions and answers below. Then, quiz a friend or family member.

How Well Do You Know _____**? A Trivia Quiz**

1. Question: _____

　　　Answer: _____

2. Question: _____

　　　Answer: _____

3. Question: _____

　　　Answer: _____

4. Question: _____

　　　Answer: _____

Name: _____ Date: _____

Collective Goals

One thing that young people have a lot of experience with is school. Yet, adults are the ones who make all the decisions. If you were in charge, what would be your goals for the schools in your state?

Directions: You have been selected to represent students at a state education committee. Prepare a presentation about the four most important issues for students in your state. List them in the boxes, and include a brief description of each issue.

Name: _____ **Date:** _____

Influences of Organizations

Every state makes its own rules about schools and education. There are a few national requirements about what and how students learn. But states, and sometimes even cities, get to make a lot of decisions for themselves.

Directions: Read the text, and answer the questions.

Foreign Languages

Only 11 states require students to study a foreign language to earn a high school diploma. Sometimes, one or two years are required, while other states require more. In some states, students can substitute other electives, such as art, for a foreign language.

1. Why do you think requirements vary so much from one state to the next?

_____

_____

_____

2. What do you think the foreign language requirement should be in your state? Why?

_____

_____

_____

3. Would you like to take foreign language courses? Why or why not?

_____

_____

_____

4. How might taking foreign language classes affect your life later?

_____

_____

_____

Focus on State
Social Awareness

Name:_____ Date:_____

Focus on State

Relationship Skills

Standing Up for Others

Students at school can sometimes be mean to one another. This can even develop into bullying behavior, which can have lasting harmful effects. You have a choice when you see this kind of mean behavior taking place. You can either be a bystander who watches and does nothing, or you can support the target of the mean behavior.

Directions: Write responses and actions for each reason a person might give for not getting involved when someone is being bullied. Then, use this outline to create a Public Service Announcement (PSA) script on a separate sheet of paper that is part of a statewide anti-bullying campaign. In your script, you should encourage people not to be bystanders.

1. Reason: "I don't want to draw attention to myself. They'll just pick on me instead."

   Encouraging Response: _____

   _____

   Suggested Action: _____

   _____

   _____

2. Reason: "Nobody would listen to me anyway."

   Encouraging Response: _____

   _____

   Suggested Action: _____

   _____

   _____

3. Reason: "It's not that bad. If we just ignore them, they'll stop."

   Encouraging Response: _____

   _____

   Suggested Action: _____

   _____

   _____

Name: _____ Date: _____

Critical-Thinking Skills

As you get older, you will gain more influence over choices that affect your life. Choosing what to do after high school is a good example. There are many factors to consider, some of which may be out of your control. For big decisions like this, it is important to weigh all factors carefully.

Directions: Your cousin is deciding where to move after graduating college. List things they should consider as they make this important choice. Then, draw what you think would be their ideal living situation.

- _____
- _____
- _____
- _____
- _____
- _____
- _____
- _____

Name: _____ Date: _____

Focus on Country

Self-Awareness

National Values

Patriotic songs tell a lot about a country's values. One such song about the United States is *America the Beautiful*. Katharine Lee Bates wrote the words in 1895. Samuel Ward first wrote the melody 12 years earlier.

Directions: Read the song. Circle all the words that show what the author values about the United States. Then, answer the questions.

America the Beautiful

Oh beautiful for spacious skies,

For amber waves of grain,

For purple mountain majesties

Above the fruited plain!

America! America!

God shed His grace on thee

And crown thy good with brotherhood

From sea to shining sea!

O beautiful for heroes proved

In liberating strife,

Who more than self their country loved

And mercy more than life!

America! America!

May God thy gold refine,

Till all success be nobleness,

And every gain divine!

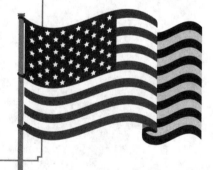

1. What values does the song show?

_____

_____

2. What would you choose to highlight in a patriotic song about the United States? Why?

_____

_____

Name: _____ **Date:** _____

Managing Emotions

You have learned how to consider the worst and best case scenarios of a situation. Countries do the same thing. They consider all the risks and think about outcomes in order to determine how to help as many people as possible.

Directions: Read the scenario. Complete the chart to show the best, worst, and most likely outcomes of the country's decision. Then, answer the question.

Huge Hurricane

There is a hurricane heading toward the southern coast of a country in three days. Scientists predict it will be the most powerful storm in 20 years. If they are correct, it could cost up to $5 billion in damages. There are 2.5 million people living in the area that will be hit hardest. It would take at least two days to evacuate the area. The cost of housing and recovery aid is unknown, but it could be enormous. The government has decided to call for mandatory evacuation.

Best-Case Outcome	Worst-Case Outcome

Most Likely Outcome

1. Do you think the country made the right choice? Why or why not?

_____

_____

Name: _____   Date: _____

Focus on Country

Social Awareness

Self-Motivation

Many students dream of playing a professional sport someday. But it takes a lot of time and effort to be one of the best in the country. According to a 2015 report, college athletes spend 30 to 40 hours a week on their sports. That's a full-time job! Imagine trying to balance that with all the other work that college demands. It's a lot!

Directions: Answer the questions.

1. What do you care enough about to become the very best? Why do you do it?

   _____

   _____

   _____

   _____

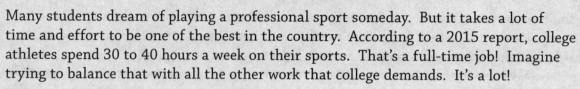

2. What would you have to sacrifice to pursue your passion? Would it be worth it? Why or why not?

   _____

   _____

   _____

   _____

3. Would you be willing to work as hard as college athletes do to reach a top level? Why or why not?

   _____

   _____

   _____

   _____

4. Why do you think these athletes work so hard and sacrifice so much?

   _____

   _____

   _____

   _____

Name: _____ Date: _____

Teamwork

Governmental leaders must work on many different teams to get things done. Some leaders work together to pass laws. Others work together to oversee departments and enforce laws and regulations. Learning how to work on a team is a valuable life skill.

Directions: Write and draw about a time you worked with a team. It might have been on a sports team, in a group project at school, or any other time you worked with others to get something done. Describe what you accomplished and how well you worked together.

_____

_____

_____

_____

_____

_____

_____

_____

_____

_____

Focus on Country

Relationship Skills

Name: _____   Date: _____

Evaluating Consequences

The United States is a huge country. Each region and state has its own problems and priorities. The federal government has to juggle all the different issues and projects that people want them to handle. They have to make choices about how to spend money and what to do first.

Directions: Read the decisions that the government could make. Answer the questions.

Cut off trade with any country that treat groups of people unfairly.

1. What are the positive consequences?

_____

_____

2. What are the negative consequences?

_____

_____

Require all citizens to serve in the military for two years after turning 18.

3. What are the positive consequences?

_____

_____

4. What are the negative consequences?

_____

_____

Offer free college education to all citizens.

5. What are the positive consequences?

_____

_____

6. What are the negative consequences?

_____

_____

Name: _____ **Date:** _____

Developing a Sense of Purpose

We all live in the same world. It's everyone's responsibility to help take care of our world and make it a better place.

Directions: Write and draw what you would like to change in the world. Include how your actions could make a difference.

What I Want to Change in the World

How I Can Make a Difference

Focus on World

Self-Awareness

Name: _____ Date: _____

Focus on World

Self-Management

Planning

Travel can be an exciting adventure. You can meet people and learn about new cultures. You can visit historical sites. You can admire arts and culture. And you can enjoy the awesome variety of nature's beauty around the world. If you plan ahead, you'll be sure to make the most out of every trip.

Directions: Imagine you have been given a year-long trip around the world. Answer the questions about how you would plan for such an adventure.

1. Where would you go? Select a few countries, and explain why you would like to visit them.

   _____

   _____

   _____

   _____

   _____

2. Plan your itinerary. Write where you will travel during each time period. Consider where countries are located to minimize travel time. Also, consider the weather at different times of the year.

   January to March

   _____

   _____

   April to June

   _____

   _____

   July to September

   _____

   _____

   October to December

   _____

   _____

Expressing Gratitude

It's easy to think of actions and words to express gratitude to a person. But what about the very planet you live on? There are so many reasons to be grateful to Earth.

Directions: Write and draw to show your gratitude for planet Earth. Then, answer the question.

What I'm Grateful For

How I Can Express My Gratitude

1. How would doing all these things make the world a better place?

_____

_____

_____

Focus on World
Social Awareness

Name: _____ Date: _____

Focus on World

Relationship Skills

Offering Support and Help

One way to build relationships between countries is to offer to help one another. Each country has its own problems, of course. But sometimes, extreme circumstances call on people to reach across borders and help each other.

Directions: Read each scenario, and answer the questions.

A country has been hit by a huge typhoon. Nearly 25 percent of the population is now homeless, and more than half the country does not have access to clean drinking water.

1. What could your country do to help?

   _____

2. What could you do to help?

   _____

A country has been fighting a civil war for more than two years. A third of the population has been forced to relocate. Food and supplies are difficult to find. The two sides are nowhere near an agreement.

3. What could your country do to help?

   _____

4. What could you do to help?

   _____

A country is experiencing its worst drought in 100 years. They are unable to grow food. The country is too poor to import enough food to feed the entire population. Famine is widespread, and people are dying of hunger every day.

5. What could your country do to help?

   _____

6. What could you do to help?

   _____

Name: _____ **Date:** _____

Identifying Causes and Effects of Conflicts

Every event is caused by some other event. Sometimes, this is intentional. The outcome may have been planned or desired. Sometimes, this is unintentional. The outcome may have been unplanned or accidental.

Directions: Answer the questions about the cause and the effects.

Cause: In the 1700s, Great Britain passed many laws raising taxes on American colonists.

Unintended Effect: American colonists declared their independence and revolted.

1. What did Great Britain intend to happen?

   _____

   _____

2. Could the British have predicted this outcome? Why or why not?

   _____

   _____

Directions: Write and draw about a time your actions had unintended effects.

Action: _____

_____

Unintended Effects: _____

_____

_____

Name:_____ Date:_____

Focus on Self

Self-Awareness

Your Digital Footprint

Think of everywhere you've ever been on the internet. Think of every piece of content you've ever posted, every comment you've ever made, and every user ID you've ever set up. These are all part of your digital footprint. It's important to be mindful of what information is out there about you, because once it's there, it's hard to remove. And almost anyone can access it.

Directions: Respond to these questions.

What online apps do you use?

_____
_____
_____
_____

What content do you post?

_____
_____
_____
_____

With whom do you interact online?

_____
_____
_____
_____

1. Review the information you posted in the footprints. Are you being thoughtful about your online presence, or do you need to be more cautious? Explain.

_____
_____
_____

Name: _____ Date: _____

Self-Discipline

Like it or not, you can't spend your entire life on screens. But regulating yourself can be tricky. Many games and websites are designed to make it difficult to stop. It's a good idea to develop strategies to help yourself monitor and limit your screen usage.

Directions: Write things you could do in each category to limit your screen usage. Circle at least two you are willing to try. Then, answer the question.

Give Myself a Reward	Fun Things to Do without a Screen

Ask for Help	Keep Track of My Screen Time

1. How do you know when you have had enough screen time?

_____

_____

Focus on Self

Self-Management

Name: _____ Date: _____

Focus on Self

Social Awareness

Understanding Different Rules

At home, you may have limits around what you can do on screens and for how long. But those rules may change once you leave your home and go to school or a friend's home. Some content or activities that are OK at home might be inappropriate elsewhere, and vice versa. It's a good idea to pay attention to what's acceptable in different situations.

Directions: Read each of the situations, and answer the questions.

1. You are in a class at school. Everyone is supposed to be using a computer to work on a writing assignment for English. Your friend next to you shows you a website that has a game with frogs and trolls. Should you check it out on your computer? Why or why not?

   _____

   _____

   _____

2. You are in the library using the computer. You really want to finish watching a movie you started streaming yesterday. But you left your headphones at home. Should you watch it anyway? Why or why not?

   _____

   _____

   _____

3. You're at home, and you finished your homework. You sit down to play a couple of quick games before dinner. Is now a good time to play? Why or why not?

   _____

   _____

   _____

4. How are the rules for using technology different at school and at home?

   _____

   _____

   _____

   _____

Name: _____ **Date:** _____

Digital Communication

The same words can have different messages. A lot depends on how the words are delivered. Your tone and the way you communicate can change the message. When you're not communicating face-to-face, you have to be even more thoughtful about how you express yourself.

Directions: Read the two messages, and answer the questions. Then, check all the items that are appropriate or necessary when communicating with adults.

1. Message to a friend: u want to go biking

   Is this appropriate communication? Why or why not?

   _____

   _____

   _____

2. Email to a teacher: what's up Ms. T what's the homework tonight? 👍

   Is this appropriate communication? Why or why not?

   _____

   _____

   _____

Communication Features

☐ abbreviations, such as lol and 4U

☐ email greetings, such as "Dear Mr. Harrison"

☐ email closings, such as "Sincerely, Tyra"

☐ emojis

☐ proper capitalization and punctuation

☐ slang

Focus on Self

Relationship Skills

Name: _____ Date: _____

Online Safety

Misusing technology can harm yourself or others. It's a good idea to ask for help from an adult when you see a use of technology that could harm someone.

Directions: Read each scenario. Write whether you should ask for help and why or why not.

1. Someone uses your secure classroom login and deletes your paper that is due tomorrow.

   _____
   _____
   _____

2. You receive a spam email asking for your personal information.

   _____
   _____
   _____

3. Someone keeps posting unflattering photos of your best friend online and then making mean comments anonymously. Everyone is talking about it at school.

   _____
   _____
   _____

4. Your password to your school website has expired. You need to make a new password to log in.

   _____
   _____
   _____

5. One of your friends posted a picture of you that you don't like.

   _____
   _____
   _____

Name: _____ Date: _____

Responding to Change

Life is full of change, especially when you are younger. Every year you grow and gain new skills. You also face new situations with new people each year. Some people thrive on change because it makes life more exciting for them. Others get stressed because they prefer the stability of a good routine. If you know how you respond to change, you can help make it as positive as possible.

Directions: Think about two times at school that you have had to deal with a big change, such as a new teacher or even a new school. Then, answer the questions about each change.

Focus on School
Self-Awareness

Change: _____

How did you feel physically?

_____

How did you feel emotionally?

_____

Did it get easier with time? If not, why not?

_____

_____

Change: _____

How did you feel physically?

_____

How did you feel emotionally?

_____

Did it get easier with time? If not, why not?

_____

_____

Name: _____ Date: _____

Focus on School

Self-Management

Planning and Organization

There are so many ways to stay organized. However, not every tool or strategy helps in every situation. With each new task at school, think about what will help you stay on track.

Directions: Draw a line from each school problem to a strategy that might help solve it.

You do your homework, but you keep losing it before turning it in.	Write assignments in a weekly planner.
You keep forgetting what is due when.	Use a phone calendar or digital home assistant to add reminders.
	Write assignments on a whiteboard at home.
You get overwhelmed by big projects and can't figure out where to start.	Divide your notebook into sections for each class.
	Ask a parent to remind you.
You get distracted by family members and don't always finish your homework.	Pack your backpack the night before.
	Break projects into smaller steps with deadlines.
You keep losing papers and materials for different subjects.	Create a quiet space to work at home.

Name: _____ Date: _____

Understanding the Influence of Organizations

School today is a lot different from how it was 100 years ago. Or even 50 years ago. The buildings are different. The teaching style is different. Even the curriculum is different. It's interesting to think about all the reasons for these changes.

Directions: Read the descriptions of dress codes in the 1920s and the 1970s and answer the questions.

1920s

Girls had to wear stockings and dresses.

Boys had to wear a hat and often had to wear short pants.

1970s

Girls had to wear skirts or dresses, unless they were wearing a matching suit jacket and pants.

Boys could not have hair that went past the ears.

1. What do you think of these rules?

_____

_____

_____

_____

2. What rules does your school have regarding a dress code?

_____

_____

_____

_____

3. Do you think your school's rules are fair? Why or why not?

_____

_____

_____

_____

Focus on School

Social Awareness

Name: _____ Date: _____

Focus on School

Relationship Skills

Building Positive Relationships

There are several ways to establish strong relationships with teachers. You don't have to pretend to be someone you're not. You just have to do your best and always try to be kind to your teachers and your classmates.

Directions: Star the strategies that are effective ways to build positive relationships with teachers. Underline any that you do.

Smile at the teacher.	Raise your hand.
Greet the teacher every day or whenever you see them.	Look at the teacher when they speak.
Rest your head on your desk.	Help your classmates when needed.
Forget to bring your materials to class.	Apologize when you get off track.
Do your assignments.	Turn your camera on for virtual learning.
Talk to your classmates during independent work time.	Thank the teacher.
Come to class late every day.	Ask questions politely.

126962—180 Days of Social-Emotional Learning

Name: _____ Date: _____

Anticipating and Evaluating Consequences

The choices you make at school often involve trade-offs. A trade-off is something you must give up in order to do something else. If you take one class, for example, you can't take another at the same time. Activities may also involve trade-offs. Sometimes, the choices you make about your social time have trade-offs, too.

Directions: Read each example of a choice. Describe the potential benefits and trade-offs created by that choice.

1. You want to join the school play. You would have to attend practice after school three days a week for two months.

Benefit	Trade-off

2. You're considering taking a higher-level math class that requires twice as much homework. But it will let you take higher-level classes in high school.

Benefit	Trade-off

3. Your teacher offers a study session after school for a difficult test. But you choose not to go.

Benefit	Trade-off

4. You usually sit with one group of friends in the cafeteria. But today, you agreed to sit with a new friend.

Benefit	Trade-off

Focus on School

Responsible Decision-Making

Focus on Community

Self-Awareness

Name: _____ Date: _____

Identifying Assets

Human-interest stories are often very popular. People like to hear about positive things that others are doing. It can also help balance the more negative news.

Directions: Your local newspaper wants to showcase stories about young people in your community. Suggest three people who would make great features. Explain your choices inside each head.

Name: _____

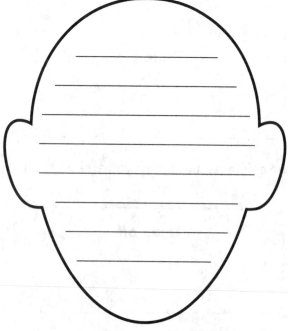

Name: _____

Name: _____

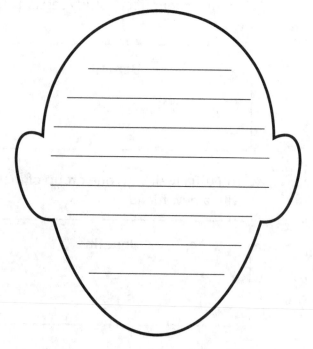

Name: _____ Date: _____

Demonstrating Personal and Collective Agency

You can be a force for good in your community. You can be proactive and take steps to help your community when you see a need. Don't wait for someone else to take care of things! There is so much that you can do yourself, even if it's just asking questions or finding other people to work with on a project.

Directions: Read the scenarios. Then, identify one thing that the characters could do to improve their communities.

1. The street leading up to Kamal's school has a long retaining wall that runs along one side of the street. It's ugly and gray. Kamal thinks it would be the perfect place for a mural, but he can't make that happen on his own.

   _____

   _____

   _____

2. Teresa hates riding the bus to school because she is the first person picked up in the morning and the last one to get off in the afternoon. It takes forever. She would like to bike to school. But there's nowhere to put her bike once she gets there.

   _____

   _____

   _____

3. Isaac has noticed a broken swing at his local playground. He's worried that a little kid is going to fall off and get hurt.

   _____

   _____

   _____

Focus on Community

Self-Management

Name: _____ Date: _____

Recognizing Others' Strengths

Your community is full of heroes. These are people who go above and beyond what is expected of them in order to make life better for others. Heroes can be found in any occupation. They can be of any age and any gender. It's worth taking a moment to appreciate your community heroes.

Directions: Imagine you are making a feel-good movie about your community. What would the storyline be? Which real people would you choose as your heroes? Why? Write a pitch to a director, that describes the story and characters and why they would be compelling to watch.

My Movie: _____

_____

_____

_____

_____

_____

_____

_____

_____

_____

_____

_____

_____

_____

_____

_____

_____

_____

Focus on Community

Social Awareness

Name: _____ Date: _____

Developing Positive Relationships

People from different age groups do not usually interact much outside their families. Children mostly play with other children. Older adults usually socialize with other adults. This is a missed opportunity. There is much wisdom to be gained from your elders. And children and young adults have a lot of energy and new ideas that should be shared with older adults.

Directions: Brainstorm ways that members of different age groups in your community could interact more. Choose two specific groups, and think of an activity that would encourage positive interaction. Then, answer the questions.

1. Which two age groups would be involved?

   _____

   _____

2. Describe the activity. What would people do? Where and when? Is it ongoing or a one-time activity?

   _____

   _____

   _____

   _____

   _____

3. What resources would you need? Who could help you find them?

   _____

   _____

   _____

4. How do you think this activity would encourage positive interactions between these two age groups?

   _____

   _____

Focus on Community

Relationship Skills

© Shell Education

Name: _____ Date: _____

Focus on Community

Responsible Decision-Making

Anticipating Consequences

Some choices that seem small can have big consequences. It's important to think about how your actions affect yourself and the rest of your community.

Directions: Describe the positive and negative consequences of each choice to yourself and to the community.

1. You leave your shopping cart loose in the parking lot.

   _____
   _____
   _____
   _____

2. You hang out in the park after dark playing flashlight tag with friends.

   _____
   _____
   _____
   _____

3. You sit and jump on the nets at the community tennis courts.

   _____
   _____
   _____
   _____
   _____

4. You and your friends play basketball and hang out on the same community court for hours.

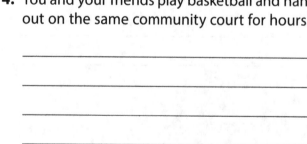

   _____
   _____
   _____
   _____
   _____

Name: _____ Date: _____

Identifying One's Emotions

States make decisions based on what is best for the people of the state as a whole. But sometimes, those decisions can have unintended consequences for smaller groups of people or individuals. Those consequences might seem unfair. They can have a big impact on your well-being and emotions.

Directions: Read the scenarios. Answer the questions.

A new state highway will go through your neighborhood. All your neighbors have to move.

1. How would this affect you?

_____

_____

2. How would this decision make you feel?

_____

_____

_____

The state has added a new graduation requirement, beginning with students in your grade.

3. How would this affect you?

_____

_____

4. How would this decision make you feel?

_____

_____

_____

Focus on State
Self-Awareness

Name: _____ Date: _____

Following the Rules

The state makes laws and regulations when necessary. They are especially needed when safety is an issue. Imagine if there were no rules. Would you feel safe?

Directions: Think about all the laws and regulations that your state government has to keep you safe. Write as many examples as you can think of in the spaces for each category. Then, put a star next to the ones that you think are most effective.

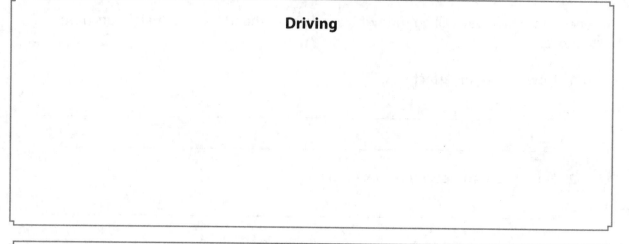

Driving

Food and Drink

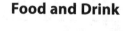

Tools and Technology

Name: _____ Date: _____

Opportunities to Improve

Have you ever seen a top 10 list on the internet or in a magazine? They include topics such as "Top 10 Best States for Families" or "Top 10 Healthiest States in America." How do you think your state would fare on a list like that?

Directions: Consider what your state needs to do to become a top-10 state where everyone would want to live. How can you help make your state safer, cleaner, or kinder? List things your state needs to improve in the first box. List things you can do to improve it in the second box.

Focus on State

Social Awareness

Needs Improvement in My State

Actions I Can Take to Improve My State

Name: _____ Date: _____

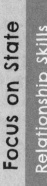

Focus on State

Relationship Skills

Developing Positive Relationships

Most young people don't get a chance to meet people from other parts of the state. When you do have an opportunity, it can be rewarding. You'll get a different perspective and maybe even break some stereotypes. The first step can be as simple as starting a conversation.

Directions: Write what the person could do in each situation to make a connection.

1. Myriam arrives at summer camp for the first time. It's an hour away from her home, so there are kids from all over the state there. She finds her cabin and sees two of her cabinmates sitting on the front steps, talking.

   _____

   _____

   _____

2. Marco is excited. He worked hard on his audition for the statewide junior band workshop and concert. And he made it. Today is the day! He's feeling nervous about the performance. What if everyone is much better than him? He walks into the orientation room. It's full of kids wandering around with their instruments.

   _____

   _____

   _____

3. Gigi is on vacation with her family. They're camping at a state park two hours from home. The campground is awesome. It has a lake for swimming and a game room for kids! Gigi's parents are settled on the beach at the lake. She's ready to have fun!

   _____

   _____

   _____

Name:_____ Date:_____

Weighing Options

You probably don't sit down to write a list of pros and cons for every decision you make. That would take too long! But pros and cons lists can be useful for big decisions. Plus, with practice, it can become an automatic process you do in your head before you make big decisions.

Directions: You can either choose to live in the biggest city in your state or one of the smallest towns. Use what you already know, and do research online. List the pros and cons for each choice. Then, answer the question.

Biggest City	
Pros	**Cons**

Smallest Town	
Pros	**Cons**

1. Choose where you want to live, and explain your reasoning using information from your pro/con charts.

_____

_____

Name:_____ Date:_____

Focus on Country

Self-Awareness

Character Traits

Stories are a great way to learn more about character traits. Authors include them in texts to help you connect with the characters or content. Historians even include them to paint a picture of historical figures. The stories are often untrue, but are meant to teach a lesson.

Directions: Read the adaptation of the fable about George Washington and the cherry tree. Then, answer the questions.

The Cherry Tree

As a young child, George Washington was given a hatchet as a present. George was eager to use his hatchet, so he tested it out on his father's prized cherry tree. Unfortunately, it worked too well, and the tree fell. George's father was angry when he saw the tree, but George confessed right away. "I cannot tell a lie," he said, and his father forgave him.

1. What character trait does this story highlight about George Washington?

_____

2. Rewrite the story focusing on Washington's father. Select a different positive character trait to highlight.

Character Trait: _____

_____

_____

_____

_____

_____

_____

_____

_____

_____

_____

_____

Name: _____ **Date:** _____

Integrity

Abraham Lincoln is often regarded as an example of an honest politician. His nickname, after all, is Honest Abe. But he was more than honest. He had integrity. *Integrity* is having consistent values and principles that you do your best to follow.

Directions: Read the following excerpt from a letter that Abraham Lincoln wrote to Major General Joseph Hooker. It explains why Lincoln chose Hooker to be the head of the Army of the Potomac. Then, answer the questions.

> "I have placed you at the head of the Army of the Potomac. Of course I have done this upon what appear to me to be sufficient reasons, and yet I think it best for you to know that there are some things in regard to which I am not quite satisfied with you. I believe you to be a brave and a skillful soldier, which of course I like…. I have heard, in such a way as to believe it, of your recently saying that both the army and the government needed a dictator. Of course it was not for this, but in spite of it, that I have given you the command. Only those generals who gain successes can set up dictators. What I now ask of you is military success, and I will risk the dictatorship."
>
> ——Abraham Lincoln

1. Why did Lincoln hire Major General Hooker?

_____

_____

2. What did Lincoln criticize about him?

_____

_____

3. How do you think this letter shows Lincoln's integrity? Use excerpts from the letter as evidence.

_____

_____

_____

_____

_____

_____

Name: _____ Date: _____

Focus on Country

Social Awareness

Recognizing Others' Strengths

Every state in the United States has a lot to admire and enjoy. Some states have vast wilderness areas to explore. Some states have large cities with great restaurants and events. Living in a different state can give you a fresh sense of perspective.

Directions: Select a state that seems completely different from your own. Research your state and the state you chose. Find information on both states in two of these categories. Then, complete the chart, and answer the questions.

Categories

air pollution	life expectancy
cost of living	number of families with children
crime rate	quality of education

	My State:	Other State:
Category:		
Category:		

1. Which state looks like it would be better for families? Why?

   _____

   _____

2. Where would you rather live, your current state or the other state? Why?

   _____

   _____

Name: _____ Date: _____

Nonverbal Communication

Nonverbal communication is a powerful tool. Politicians know this, which is how political ads can send strong messages without words. They choose visuals to set a certain mood. They use characters and actions to tell a story. And they choose sounds and music to set the right tone.

Directions: Read these two versions of a political advertisement with the same verbal messages. Underline or highlight all the nonverbal cues in each script. Then, answer the questions.

Version 1

The ad begins in front of a stereotypical suburban home with a white picket fence. The sun is shining, and birds are chirping. Children ride by on their bikes, laughing. A friendly voice says, "You value the safety and happiness of your family. You care about your community. So does Susan Weinberg." The ad ends zoomed in on a happy family with their dog.

Version 2

The ad begins in a dark, dirty alley. A child stands up in the corner with a skinny dog. He looks scared. Eerie music begins. It starts quietly and slowly gets louder. The child starts walking out of the alley, looking around nervously. A low, creepy voice begins talking. "You value the safety and happiness of your family. You care about your community. So does Susan Weinberg." The ad ends zoomed in on the child, as he holds his shaking dog.

1. What was the main point of the verbal message in both ads?

   _____

   _____

   _____

   _____

2. How are the nonverbal messages different in the two ads?

   _____

   _____

   _____

   _____

Name: _____ Date: _____

Focus on Country

Responsible Decision-Making

Identifying Solutions

You may have heard about the rivalry between Aaron Burr and Alexander Hamilton. Maybe you've seen the musical *Hamilton*. Maybe you learned about their duel in history class. They never got along. They often fought over political positions. But why were they so upset with each other in the end? And could they have avoided the final, deadly outcome?

Directions: Read the summary of the final conflict between Aaron Burr and Alexander Hamilton. Then, answer the questions.

Burr and Hamilton

Aaron Burr and Alexander Hamilton were political rivals for many years. In the end, Burr killed Hamilton in a duel. Why were they dueling? It was supposedly all about an insult Hamilton made about Burr at a party. It's like a game of telephone gone bad. Someone told Burr that Hamilton said something truly awful about him. Burr demanded an apology. Hamilton refused. The letters went back and forth until Burr decided he could only reclaim his reputation by fighting a duel. Hamilton reluctantly agreed.

1. Imagine you were Hamilton's friend. What would you advise him to do to prevent the duel?

   _____

   _____

   _____

2. Imagine you were Burr's friend. What would you advise him to do to prevent the duel?

   _____

   _____

   _____

Aaron Burr

Alexander Hamilton

Name:_____ Date:_____

Appreciating the World

Songs and poems can be effective ways to pay tribute to someone or something that you love. Louis Armstrong sang the famous song, "What a Wonderful World," about all the wonderful things he sees in the world. Some of them are physical things, such as trees, roses, blue skies, and the colors of the rainbow. Others are heartwarming scenes with people. He describes "friends shaking hands, saying 'How do you do?' They're really saying, 'I love you.'" What would you include if you wrote a tribute to the world?

Directions: Write lyrics to a song called "My Wonderful World."

My Wonderful World

_____

_____

_____

_____

_____

_____

_____

_____

_____

_____

_____

_____

_____

_____

_____

_____

_____

_____

Focus on World

Self-Awareness

Name: _____ Date: _____

Focus on World

Self-Management

Taking Action

The world is a big place, but that doesn't mean you can't make a difference. Everyone has the power and the responsibility to help make the world a better place.

Directions: Identify at least one thing each person could do to improve the world.

1. Jonny learned about climate change in science class. He was horrified to hear that polar bears and penguins are losing their habitats as the polar caps melt more and more. He's been passionate about penguins since he was in preschool. But he wonders what a kid in the United States can do about penguin habitats.

   _____

   _____

   _____

2. Kelly and Vanita are in scouts together. At last night's meeting, they learned that some American soldiers are stationed abroad for years at a time. They can't come home for holidays. Sometimes, they can't even talk to their families on the phone. It's almost Thanksgiving, and Kelly and Vanita want to do something to cheer up the soldiers who are far from home.

   _____

   _____

   _____

3. There are several refugee families in Laverne's church who are from the same country. Laverne has heard them speak multiple times about how hard things are for their families back in their homeland. Then, her class talked about that country today in school. There has been war in that country for more than three years. Many homes have been destroyed, and many people are starving.

   _____

   _____

   _____

Name:_____ Date:_____

Recognizing Others' Strengths

Every country is unique. They may not all be the biggest or the most populous. But every nation can claim something special and distinctive.

Directions: Many school yearbooks include awards that are voted on by the students. Examples include: Best Smile, Most Likely to Succeed, and Funniest. Create a list like this for countries. You can use the example categories, or make up your own. They can be serious or silly. Once you've chosen four categories, research online to find which country should win each award.

Example Categories

highest chocolate consumption   most lions

highest population   most movies watched per person

largest land area   most trees

Category: _____

Country: _____

This country deserves this award because:

_____
_____
_____
_____

Category: _____

Country: _____

This country deserves this award because:

_____
_____
_____
_____

Category: _____

Country: _____

This country deserves this award because:

_____
_____
_____
_____

Category: _____

Country: _____

This country deserves this award because:

_____
_____
_____
_____

Focus on World
Social Awareness

Name: _____ Date: _____

Focus on World
Relationship Skills

Diplomacy

Diplomacy is the art of building relationships. It often happens between countries as they work to solve problems peacefully. It's very tricky. Language barriers make it hard. Cultural differences also make it challenging. What is normal in one place may seem strange somewhere else. Countries use rules to help make diplomacy work.

Directions: Read the examples of diplomatic rules. Then, answer the questions.

Diplomatic Rules

Representatives of countries follow strict rules for diplomacy. This includes how to greet people, in what order to introduce them, and where to seat people. It also includes whether or not to shake hands, who gives toasts, who gives speeches, and what to wear. There are many other rules that are specific to each country.

1. What is the point of all these rules?

   _____

   _____

   _____

2. Do you think diplomatic rules help improve relations between countries? Why or why not?

   _____

   _____

   _____

3. Should there be clear rules like this for everyday interactions between individuals, too? Why or why not?

   _____

   _____

   _____

Name: _____ Date: _____

Evaluating Consequences

Not acting is a choice by itself. *Inaction*, which is doing nothing, means you are giving up control and allowing someone or something else to direct what happens next. Sometimes, that is the right decision. Other times, it causes more problems.

Directions: Read each situation. Write what would happen if the countries did nothing. Then, list a different choice they could make and the consequences of that choice.

1. A natural disaster has left thousands of people without homes or jobs.

Choice	Consequences
Do nothing.	

Choice	Consequences

2. There are millions of refugees in the world. Many of them are stuck in unhealthy situations such as refugee camps. They may lack access to clean water or sufficient food.

Choice	Consequences
Do nothing.	

Choice	Consequences

Focus on World

Responsible Decision-Making

Answer Key

There are many open-ended pages and writing prompts in this book. For those activities, the answers will vary. Examples are given as needed.

Week 1 Day 3 (page 14)
Examples:

1. The people are upset; they are yelling, and their brows are furrowed.
2. The person getting made fun of is upset and sad. He is frowning and hunching.
3. Both people are happy and excited; they are smiling.

Week 1 Day 5 (page 16)
1. Small Problem
2. Big Problem
3. Big Problem
4. Big Problem
5. Big Problem

Week 2 Day 1 (page 17)
Examples:

1. Negative; I will probably get in trouble
2. Positive; my sister will be grateful and happy
3. Negative; the problem won't go away. I'll get in trouble, and I won't have a bike
4. Positive; it will probably make my family member happy

Week 2 Day 2 (page 18)
Examples:

1. Worse; it makes me feel like I'm treated unfairly.
2. Worse; it makes me feel like my parents are mean.
3. Better; it might solve my problem.

Week 2 Day 3 (page 19)
Examples:

1. Maria could ask her brother what's wrong and offer to help.
2. Jamie could offer to help fix her mother's mug, or just comfort her so she feels better.
3. Will can find a quiet activity to do alone while his grandpa rests.
4. He could go find Dana and apologize for teasing her.

Week 2 Day 5 (page 21)
Examples:

1. Negative; I'll have to beg for help, or my project might be late.

   Classmate: negative; whoever I ask for help may be annoyed, or they might not have time to help right now.
2. Positive; I'll get more rest and won't feel rushed in the morning.

   Parent: positive; they will be impressed at my responsibility and relieved that they don't have to remind me.
3. Positive; I'll get some good advice.

   Friend: positive; this might help repair our relationship.

Week 3 Day 4 (page 25)
Examples:

1. Benji could bring a comic book and show it to Phuong at lunch.
2. Kara could join Mrs. Ellicott at the park one day and ask to help her feed the pigeons.
3. Gina could ask to bring her puppy over to play.

Week 4 Day 4 (page 30)
Examples:

1. I could make and post a sign about respect and compassion. I could read a book about racism.
2. I could join an anti-racist group. I could talk to my friends about what happened.

Week 5 Day 3 (page 34)
Examples:

1. Laura could send them a letter or call them to see how they are doing. She could invite them to come visit her. She could send them a care package of goodies.
2. Yousef could call them or send a card or a care package.
3. Dan could send his uncle a card. He could invite him to visit. He could offer to hold onto anything valuable for him.

Week 5 Day 4 (page 35)
Examples: intelligent, good speaker, visionary, strong morals, brave, confident

Answer Key (cont.)

Week 5 Day 5 (page 36)

Examples:

Pros: If elected, they will get to make a difference, they can get people excited about issues they care about, they will get to talk to other leaders, they will talk to many people around the country.

Cons: They may not win, it is expensive to run, the media will follow them around, it will be a hard job even if they win.

Week 6 Day 1 (page 37)

Examples:

Do: eat, sleep, drink, have fun

Want: people to care about them, fun things to do

Need: food, shelter, sleep, water, love

Feel: happy, sad, nervous, angry, worried

1. Example: It's a good reminder that we actually have a lot in common. It makes the world feel like a much smaller place.

Week 6 Day 2 (page 38)

Examples:

1. Global Problem; write to my representative about global warming.
2. Local Problem; pick up trash, and speak up when I see someone littering.
3. Local Problem; talk to my school about organizing events on mental health.
4. Global Problem; organize a fundraiser for an organization that helps refugees.

Week 6 Day 4 (page 40)

1. Jody must have misunderstood what she was ordering. Raw beef is a delicacy in France.
2. Liam's mom didn't know about the Islamic observance of Ramadan, which requires Muslims to fast during daylight hours.
3. Pointing is sometimes acceptable in the United States, but it is rude in his culture.

Week 6 Day 5 (page 41)

1. Authoritarian
2. Compromising
3. Authoritarian
4. Example: Compromising works better because all parties can be mostly satisfied.
5. Example: Authoritarian solutions might be useful in an emergency because they are fast.

Week 7 Day 3 (page 44)

1. My friend might feel sad that she didn't win and has no family there.
2. The rest of the team probably feels proud and excited because they just won the state championship and played a great game.
3. The teacher might feel disappointed because I did so poorly and didn't seem grateful to retake the test.
4. My friend might feel left out or jealous because they can't play this game.

Week 7 Day 4 (page 45)

1. Jayden feels worried or disappointed; eyes are scrunched together, sighs loudly, puts his head down, shrugs.
2. Cece seems annoyed or angry; sharp tone, rolls her eyes, turns her back away, spins around, just looks, storms off.
3. They feel happy to be together and happy to see me; smile, lean close, whisper, high five.

Week 8 Day 1 (page 47)

1. Elena already has plans with Sophie, but she wants to accept an invitation from another friend. To do that, she would have to cancel on Sophie.
2. Example: She would cancel her plans with Sophie and go to the slumber party. She would probably feel excited at first but also guilty and ashamed for canceling.
3. Example: She would keep her plans with Sophie. She would feel good about herself as a person for being a good friend.

Week 8 Day 3 (page 49)

Examples:

1. Verbal: "That stinks! You didn't even get to enjoy it yet."

   Nonverbal: Look him in the eyes while he talks, and listen carefully.
2. Verbal: "Oh no! Do you want some help cleaning up?"

   Nonverbal: Help her pick things up, and walk her to the bathroom to clean up.
3. Verbal: "I can't believe you didn't make it. I know you worked really hard."

   Nonverbal: Give her a hug and a sympathetic look.

Answer Key (cont.)

Week 8 Day 4 (page 50)

Examples:

1. He could ask Sam about what happened.
2. She could ask her friends why they didn't invite her.
3. Tyler could ask Jen what happened.

Week 8 Day 5 (page 51)

Best for Lucas: to do the project on Argentina

Best for His Friends: to do the project on Italy so they can make pizza

Best for the Group: to do the project on Argentina because they would have more resources

Week 9 Day 1 (page 52)

Examples:

1. They think we are irresponsible or immature.
2. Adults forget what it's like to be a kid.
3. Volunteer projects, performances, academic achievements, etc.
4. These events might help someone appreciate a culture that they didn't understand before.

Week 9 Day 2 (page 53)

Examples:

1. Bring a trash bag with them, and pick up trash on the way to the park.
2. Contact the Parks and Recreation Department, and ask them to fix the court.
3. Offer to shovel Rose's sidewalk, and organize friends to shovel more.

Week 10 Day 2 (page 58)

1. Create a method for towns and cities to report if their greenhouse gas emissions have gone down.
2. Give people incentives to use less energy.
3. Reduce energy use by 20 percent in the summer.

Week 11 Day 1 (page 62)

Core values may include equality, rights, and freedom.

Week 12 Day 4 (page 70)

Examples:

1. The countries can each build a canal from the river.
2. One country takes all the resources and leaves nothing for the other.
3. All three countries continue to fish as much as they can.
4. No, sometimes there aren't enough resources for a win-win, or the demands of one side are too unreasonable for everyone to be happy.

Week 12 Day 5 (page 71)

Two countries both claim the same city as their own: Failed negotiations lead to war.

Multiple countries want control over unclaimed islands that have a lot of valuable resources: An uninvolved country hosts negotiations to find a way to share resources.

One country's navy accidentally sinks an innocent fishing boat from another country: An apology is offered and accepted quickly. Money is sent in compensation.

Thousands of refugees from one country have flooded into another country: Other countries offer support and help build temporary shelters.

1. Apologies, successful negotiations, and the help of other countries led to positive outcomes.
2. Failed negotiations led to war.

Week 13 Day 5 (page 76)

Examples:

1. He thinks the idea sounds like a lot of fun.
2. "Hmmm, that might be fun. Give me a second to think about it."
3. Why are the other people standing near the baseball diamond? Is there a practice or game starting soon?
4. Leon and his friends would be disappointed. Leon might feel guilty, and his friends might be annoyed that they came all the way over for nothing because others are using the field.

Answer Key (cont.)

Week 14 Day 2 (page 78)
Example:

Monday: Finish novel after school. Study for math test after dinner.

Tuesday: Complete social studies project, and start art project.

Wednesday: Complete science questions, and work on art project.

Thursday: Finish art project.

Week 14 Day 4 (page 80)
1. No; no; no

   The teacher will probably be annoyed because it sounds like they weren't paying attention.

2. Yes; yes; yes

   The teacher will probably be happy to help because the student is trying hard.

3. Yes; yes; yes

   The teacher will probably be happy to help because the student is trying hard.

Week 15 Day 3 (page 84)
Examples:

Teachers: blamed when people are focusing on the poor test scores, but appreciative of funding

High school students: frustrated about the lack of support for a new building

Parents: frustrated that the building is in bad condition and that the test scores are so low

Community members without children: frustrated about the cost of either proposal, since it will come out of their taxes

Week 15 Day 4 (page 85)
1. No, because it does not admit responsibility.
2. No, because it makes excuses.
3. Yes, because it admits responsibility and doesn't make excuses.
4. No, because it makes excuses.
5. Yes, because it admits responsibility and doesn't make excuses.

Week 15 Day 5 (page 86)
Examples:

1. Positive: The intersection will be safer.

   Negative: It may take longer to get places.

2. Positive: Skaters will have a safe place to skate.

   Negative: It could get noisy.

3. Positive: People who want to raise chickens will be able to.

   Negative: The smell and noise may bother neighbors.

Week 16 Day 3 (page 89)
Examples:

1. Yvonne is used to riding the bus and going to the corner store because she's been doing that for years. Many places are closer together in a city. But cities have higher crime rates, so maybe that's why her parents don't want her to be home alone.

2. There's little public transportation in the suburbs and most places are too far for Ruthie to walk or bike to. But crime rates are probably low, so she's allowed to stay home alone.

3. In a rural community, everybody knows everybody. So, Ishaan's parents probably worry less about where he is during the day. He might have more freedom, but there aren't too many places he can go.

Week 16 Day 4 (page 90)
Examples:

1. Sam could write to his representatives and educate himself more by reading about migrant workers.

2. Sam could ask his teacher to invite a guest speaker to class to talk about migrant workers and create a flyer explaining how migrant workers live.

Week 17 Day 3 (page 94)
Examples:

1. I can choose which house of worship I go to, or I can choose not to go.
2. I can choose my doctors and my schools.
3. I can feel safe taking medicine, knowing that it won't harm me.
4. I can breathe more easily because the air is not as polluted as it might be.
5. I can criticize a person or a law and will not be punished.
6. I can go to school and get an education.

Answer Key *(cont.)*

Week 17 Day 4 (page 95)

Examples:

1. This seems like a fair compromise because they both got something that they wanted.
2. This doesn't seem fair because 18 percent is not halfway between 10 percent and 20 percent. But there are more people in the first group, so they have more influence.

Week 17 Day 5 (page 96)

Examples:

1. It kept the land near them preserved.
2. It gave them new places to vacation and explore the wilderness.
3. It protected the plants and animals living in the national park areas.
4. It probably increased tourism in the areas around the national parks, so other businesses, such as hotels and restaurants, probably saw an increase as well.
5. Yes, because it generally benefitted everyone.

Week 18 Day 5 (page 101)

Examples:

1. More people will live longer in those countries.
2. Immigrants may try to enter illegally, businesses may not have enough specialized workers, families may not be able to reunite.
3. People might not be able to get the goods they want, prices might increase.
4. There might be too many people who want to live in some countries.
5. Air pollution would improve.

Week 19 Day 4 (page 105)

1. Underline: Stop being so lazy! You're driving me crazy!

   Example: I am feeling frustrated because we have a lot to do. I would appreciate it if you could help me.
2. Underline: You're giving me a headache!

   Example: I would appreciate it if you could quiet down because I have a bad headache.
3. Underline: You ruined my bike! You're so irresponsible!

   Example: I am upset about the dent and the flat tire. I would appreciate it if you could help fix it for me.
4. Underline: You ate the last one? You're so rude!

   Example: I'm disappointed that I didn't get to try any cookies. Can we ask your mom if she can make some more?

Week 20 Day 2 (page 108)

1. B
2. B
3. A

All the helpful messages acknowledge the problem but also express a more positive way to look at the situation.

Week 20 Day 3 (page 109)

I should choose the 3:00 p.m. movie. The earlier shows conflict with the soccer game and doctor's appointment. The later times would conflict with my parents' plans for the evening.

Week 20 Day 4 (page 110)

Helpers: nodding to show agreement, smiling, speaking clearly

Blockers: avoiding eye contact, interrupting, looking at your phone while someone is talking, not responding, mumbling, rolling your eyes

Week 20 Day 5 (page 111)

1. Taylor doesn't know whether she should open the door because she's home alone.
2. She needs to know if there's an emergency and if the man is really from the gas company.
3. She could call a parent for advice or contact the gas company.
4. She should call her parent or another trusted adult because she should not talk to the person at the door unless she's sure it's safe.

Answer Key (cont.)

Week 21 Day 4 (page 115)

Examples:

1. "You might not realize this, but some of the snow from your driveway is getting blown onto mine. Could you please aim it somewhere else?"
2. "Uh oh! Your dog ran through my flower beds. Can you help me clean this up?"
3. "Excuse me, Mr. Frank, I need to get out of my driveway for an urgent appointment. Could you please move your car?"

Week 21 Day 5 (page 116)

1. The hunters want to hunt in the conservation land. The other users want to be able to use the land safely.
2. Example: There could be specific times designated for hunting each day during hunting seasons. At other times, it would not be allowed.
3. Both groups want to be in the same place at the same time.
4. Example: They could trade off weeks, or one could find another space in the library.

Week 22 Day 2 (page 118)

Examples:

Self-Talk: remind herself that she is prepared and that yesterday was a fluke.

Mindfulness Techniques: close her eyes and focus on her breathing; meditate

Things That Make Her Happy: listen to her favorite song; talk to a supportive friend

Week 22 Day 3 (page 119)

Examples:

1. I would feel excited to have an airport so close to home.
2. They would feel disappointed and might even think the decision was unfair. The train would have been convenient for them.
3. I would have felt disappointed.
4. I would hope the people in the two major cities were respectful of my feelings.

Week 22 Day 5 (page 121)

Examples:

1. Workers who earn minimum wage would earn more.
2. Business would have to pay more, so they might raise prices.
3. Kids might be safer at home at night.
4. Kids would not be able to do extracurricular activities in the evenings.

Week 23 Day 3 (page 124)

Examples:

Reasons to Come: new economic opportunities, better life for themselves and their children, educational opportunities, escaping violence or hardship back home

Personal Challenges on Arrival: learning a new language, learning a new culture, not knowing anyone, possibly not having much money, finding a new job

Benefits to Society: new perspectives, workers with expertise, hard workers, excellent students and researchers, new friends, new taxpayers

Week 24 Day 3 (page 129)

Examples:

1. They might feel nervous and scared because the government is gone and they don't know what will happen next.
2. They might feel happy, but people in their neighboring countries might be jealous or resentful that they aren't helping.
3. They might be very scared because they are in the middle of an army and can't go anywhere.
4. Residents might feel annoyed that their country has to pay to help the refugees, or they might feel compassionate and want to help. The refugees would probably feel scared and wonder if they will ever get to go home, or they might feel hopeful of being allowed to stay.

Week 24 Day 5 (page 131)

1. high-level; there are many countries involved and it's complicated.
2. low-level; they are generally in agreement and just need to decide details.
3. high-level; it affects all countries, and is urgent.

Answer Key (cont.)

Week 25 Day 1 (page 132)

1. fixed mindset

   Example: Remind himself that he usually passes the tests without even trying much, so if he tried, he might do great.

2. fixed mindset

   Example: Tell herself that every sport is different, and second grade was a long time ago. Plus, plenty of people just do sports for fun.

3. growth mindset

   Example: Work with his brother some more to get even more confident at writing.

Week 25 Day 3 (page 134)

Examples:

1. Her father feels disappointed and sad because he wanted it to be a special treat.

2. She could thank her dad for working so hard on her dessert and give him a big hug.

3. She's very sad that her cat died.

4. Kate could give her a hug and ask her about her favorite memories of the cat.

Week 25 Day 5 (page 136)

1. ignore it; destructive

2. get help from a friend, study instead of attend a party; constructive

3. give in to his friends; destructive

4. stay up late to read a book; destructive

Week 26 Day 2 (page 138)

Examples:

1. I have a great time and make new friends.

2. I feel awkward or say something silly and nobody talks to me.

3. The best case is more likely. It's unlikely that no one will talk to me.

4. It's better to go to the party because I will probably have a good time.

Week 26 Day 3 (page 139)

Examples:

Parker & Aaron: We weren't trying to be mean. It's just that we have a lot in common with the other hockey guys. We weren't laughing at Rafael. He's a nice guy.

Rafael: I don't know why they're trying to ditch me. I thought we were friends. Did I do something wrong? Why are they being so mean to me?

1. Nobody is really wrong, but they should still try to communicate better with each other.

Week 26 Day 4 (page 140)

1. Blaming words: it's all your fault, blaming this on me

2. Accusing words: you told them, you never believe anything I say

3. Insults: worst friend ever, jerk

4. Example: "Whitney, did you tell them about the math test? Everybody was making fun of me, and it felt terrible."
   "No, Lisa, I didn't say anything. They heard Timmy talking about it at recess. I'm so sorry that happened!"

Week 27 Day 4 (page 145)

1. passive-aggressive

2. assertive

3. passive-aggressive

4. passive-aggressive

Week 28 Day 4 (page 150)

Examples:

1. Encouraging Response: If nobody stands up to them, they'll continue to pick on others, like you.

   Suggested Action: Say something such as, "Stop it, that's not cool," or offer help to the target.

2. Encouraging Response: It might feel like you're powerless, but you're not!

   Suggested Action: Find a friend or two to stand up with you.

3. Encouraging Response: It's easier to stop before it gets that bad. They might not stop.

   Suggested Action: If it's something small, try using humor to stop them.

Week 29 Day 2 (page 153)

Examples:

Best Case: Thousands of lives will be saved. People will be able to go home quickly and easily.

Worst Case: It could cost a huge amount of money to coordinate the evacuation and provide temporary housing for people. It might take weeks before everyone can go home again. Or the storm might not hit at all, and it will all be wasted time and effort.

Most Likely: It will cost thousands to evacuate and house people, but they will probably be able to return home in a few days if the damage is not too extensive.

Answer Key *(cont.)*

Week 29 Day 5 (page 156)

Examples:

1. It might put pressure on those countries to expand opportunities and freedoms for repressed groups.
2. People might be missing goods from those countries, and it might cause those countries to be less willing to change their ways.
3. There would be plenty of recruits in the military.
4. Many people don't want to serve in the military. If there is a war, they would be forced to fight.
5. More people would enroll in college and have more education.
6. It would cost a lot of money and might require higher taxes.

Week 30 Day 4 (page 160)

Example:

1. They could send drinking water and engineers to help clean up the water supply. They could send money to build shelters or homes.
2. I could donate money or supplies.
3. They could send international mediators to help broker a peace treaty. They could send humanitarian aid and food.
4. I could donate to an organization that helps people in that country. I could tell my friends about it.
5. They could send food and technical assistance to help end the effects of the drought.
6. I could donate money and organize a fundraiser at my school.

Week 30 Day 5 (page 161)

Examples:

1. Britain wanted to raise more money and remind the colonists who was in charge.
2. They could have predicted it based on the response to earlier taxes.

Week 31 Day 2 (page 163)

Examples:

Give Myself a Reward: homemade brownies every week that I spend less time playing video games; a new board game or other screen-free prize

Fun Things to Do without a Screen: ride my bike, make a dessert, craft, play a sport

Ask for Help: ask my parent to set up limits on my screen usage and remind me; find a friend to do a new activity with me

Keep Track of My Screen Time: keep a journal of screen usage so I can see how much time I really spend on it; set a timer so I quit in time

Week 31 Day 4 (page 165)

1. Yes, communication between friends can be casual.
2. No, there is no greeting, it's too informal, it uses slang, and there is no capitalization or punctuation.

Check: email greetings, email closings, proper capitalization and punctuation

Week 31 Day 5 (page 166)

Examples:

1. Yes, because your paper is due tomorrow. They may be able to recover your file.
2. No, because you can just delete spam emails.
3. Yes, because this is cyberbullying. It needs to be addressed or it can do serious harm to your friend.
4. No, because you can create a new password on your own.
5. No, because you can just ask them to take it down first.

Week 32 Day 4 (page 170)

Starred: Smile at the teacher, Greet the teacher every day, Do your assignments, Ask questions politely, Raise your hand, Look at the teacher when they speak, Help your classmates when needed, Apologize when you get off track, Speak to classmates politely, Thank the teacher, Ask questions politely

Answer Key (cont.)

Week 32 Day 5 (page 171)

Examples:

1. Benefits: it would be fun, get experience in theater, make new friends

   Trade-offs: can't do anything else after school, have to budget time wisely

2. Benefits: it may give me more academic and career opportunities

   Trade-offs: homework would take a lot of time, and it will be harder

3. Benefits: have more time to do other fun things

   Trade-offs: might not do as well on the test

4. Benefits: get to know a new friend

   Trade-offs: might upset my old friends, might not be invited back

Week 33 Day 2 (page 173)

Examples:

1. Kamal could ask his art teacher if they could organize a group to paint a mural.

2. Teresa could talk to her principal about raising money to put in a bike rack at the school.

3. Isaac could call the Parks and Recreation Department and ask them to fix the swing. Until then, he could put up a warning sign on the swing.

Week 33 Day 5 (page 176)

Examples:

1. I can get out of the parking lot a little faster, but someone might complain to me; it might roll and hit someone's car or cause an accident.

2. I might have fun, but I could also get in trouble for being in the park after closing. I might also injure myself. Neighbors might be scared when they see lights in the park; they might call the police.

3. I might have fun, but I could also get in trouble; the nets might break, and then the community will have to repair them. Nobody will be able to use them in the meantime.

4. I might have fun and get better at basketball, but no one else would be able to use the court and people might complain.

Week 34 Day 4 (page 180)

Examples:

1. She could approach them and introduce herself as another member of their cabin.

2. He could look for people he knows or people who play the same instrument. That would give him something they have in common that he could mention when he says hello.

3. She could start swimming and look for kids who are near her age playing in the water. Or she could go to the game room and introduce herself.

Week 35 Day 2 (page 183)

1. He is a brave and skillful soldier.

2. Hooker said the army and the government needed a dictator.

3. Lincoln was honest about what he liked and didn't like. He admitted that Hooker did not share all his values, but warned him that he wouldn't change Lincoln's mind.

Week 35 Day 4 (page 185)

1. Susan Weinberg cares about the safety and happiness of your family and community.

2. The message in the first ad is that things are great, and Susan Weinberg will help keep them that way. The message in the second ad is that there are a lot of scary things out there, and Susan Weinberg will help protect you.

Week 36 Day 2 (page 188)

Examples:

1. He can organize a fundraiser for an environmental group that is working to protect the Arctic.

2. They could ask their scout troop to create cards and care packages to send to the soldiers for Thanksgiving.

3. She could organize a clothing and food drive to send supplies over to people in that country.

Week 36 Day 4 (page 190)

Examples:

1. The rules make interactions predictable to avoid miscommunication, which lets countries focus on the issues they want to solve.

2. Yes, because misunderstandings could have a huge effect when there's a conflict between powerful countries. Following diplomatic rules is a way of showing respect for the other.

3. No, because people within a culture often already follow unwritten rules.

References Cited

The Aspen Institute: National Commission on Social, Emotional, & Academic Development. 2018. "From a Nation at Risk to a Nation at Hope." https://nationathope.org/wp-content/uploads/2018_aspen_final-report_full_webversion.pdf.

Collaborative for Academic, Social, and Emotional Learning (CASEL). n.d. "What Is SEL?" Last modified December 2020. https://casel.org/what-is-sel/.

Durlak, Joseph A., Roger P. Weissberg, Allison B. Dymnicki, Rebecca D. Taylor, and Kriston B. Schellinger. 2011. "The Impact of Enhancing Students' Social and Emotional Learning: A Meta-Analysis of School-Based Universal Interventions." *Child Development* 82 (1): 405–32.

Goleman, Daniel. 2005. *Emotional Intelligence: Why It Can Matter More Than IQ.* New York: Bantam Dell.

Palmer, Parker J. 2007. *The Courage to Teach: Exploring the Inner Landscape of a Teacher's Life.* San Francisco: Jossey-Bass.

Name: _____ Date: _____

Connecting to Self Rubric

Days 1 and 2

Directions: Complete this rubric every six weeks to evaluate students' Day 1 and Day 2 activity sheets. Only one rubric is needed per student. Their work over the six weeks can be considered together. Appraise their work in each category by circling or highlighting the descriptor in each row that best describes the student's work. Then, consider the student's overall progress in connecting to self. In the box, draw ☆, ✓+ , or ✓ to indicate your overall evaluation.

Competency	Advanced	Satisfactory	Developing
Self-Awareness	Can accurately identify one's own full range of emotions.	Identifies one's own emotions accurately most of the time.	Has trouble identifying their own feelings.
	Understands that thoughts and feelings are connected.	Sees the connection of thoughts and feelings most of the time.	Does not connect thoughts to feelings.
	Can identify strengths and areas of growth.	Can identify a few strengths and weaknesses.	Can identify only one strength or weakness.
Self-Management	Can manage stress by using several different strategies.	Manages stress with only one strategy.	Does not manage stress well.
	Shows motivation in all areas of learning.	Shows motivation in a few areas of learning.	Shows little to no motivation.
	Is able to set realistic goals.	Sets some goals that are realistic and some that are not.	Has a hard time setting goals that are achievable.

Comments

_____

_____

_____

Overall

Name: _____ Date: _____

Relating to Others Rubric

Days 3 and 4

Directions: Complete this rubric every six weeks to evaluate students' Day 3 and Day 4 activity sheets. Only one rubric is needed per student. Their work over the six weeks can be considered together. Appraise their work in each category by circling or highlighting the descriptor in each row that best describes the student's work. Then, consider the student's overall progress in relating to others. In the box, draw ☆, ✓+ , or ✓ to indicate your overall evaluation.

Competency	Advanced	Satisfactory	Developing
Social Awareness	Shows empathy toward others.	Shows empathy toward others most of the time.	Shows little to no empathy toward others.
	Can explain how rules are different in different places.	Knows that some places can have different rules.	Is not able to articulate how rules may change in different places.
	Can list many people who support them in their learning.	Can list some people who support them in their learning.	Can list few people who support them in their learning.
Relationship Skills	Uses a variety of strategies to solve conflicts with peers.	Has a few strategies to solve conflicts with peers.	Struggles to solve conflicts with peers.
	Uses advanced skills of listening and paraphrasing while communicating.	Is able to communicate effectively.	Has breakdowns in communication skills.
	Works effectively with a team. Shows leadership in accomplishing team goals.	Works effectively with a team most of the time.	Has trouble working with others on a team.

Comments

Overall

_____

_____

_____

Name: _____ Date: _____

Making Decisions Rubric

Day 5

Directions: Complete this rubric every six weeks to evaluate students' Day 5 activity sheets. Only one rubric is needed per student. Their work over the six weeks can be considered together. Appraise their work in each category by circling or highlighting the descriptor in each row that best describes the student's work. Then, consider the student's overall progress in making decisions. In the box, draw ☆, ✓+, or ✓ to indicate your overall evaluation.

Competency	Advanced	Satisfactory	Developing
Responsible Decision-Making	Makes decisions that benefit their own long-term interests.	Makes decisions that are sometimes impulsive and sometimes thought out.	Is impulsive and has a hard time making constructive choices.
	Knows how to keep self and others safe in a variety of situations.	Knows how to keep themselves safe in most situations.	Is capable of being safe, but sometimes is not.
	Is able to consider the consequences of their actions, both good and bad.	Is able to identify some consequences of their actions.	Struggles to anticipate possible consequences to their actions.

Comments

_____

_____

_____

_____

Overall

Connecting to Self Analysis

Directions: Record each student's overall symbols (page 202) in the appropriate columns. At a glance, you can view: (1) which students need more help mastering these skills and (2) how students progress throughout the school year.

Student Name	Week 6	Week 12	Week 18	Week 24	Week 30	Week 36

Relating to Others Analysis

Directions: Record each student's overall symbols (page 203) in the appropriate columns. At a glance, you can view: (1) which students need more help mastering these skills and (2) how students progress throughout the school year.

Student Name	Week 6	Week 12	Week 18	Week 24	Week 30	Week 36

Making Decisions Analysis

Directions: Record each student's overall symbols (page 204) in the appropriate columns. At a glance, you can view: (1) which students need more help mastering these skills and (2) how students progress throughout the school year.

Student Name	Week 6	Week 12	Week 18	Week 24	Week 30	Week 36

126962—180 Days of Social-Emotional Learning

Digital Resources

Accessing the Digital Resources

The Digital Resources can be downloaded by following these steps:

1. Go to **www.tcmpub.com/digital**

2. Use the ISBN number to redeem the Digital Resources.

3. Respond to the question using the book.

4. Follow the prompts on the Content Cloud website to sign in or create a new account.

5. Choose the Digital Resources you would like to download. You can download all the files at once, or a specific group of files.

ISBN: 9781087649757